The Leadership Platform

A practical guide to building a strong and effective leadership foundation

Jim Hessler
with Steve Motenko

Copyright © 2008 Path Foward

All rights reserved. No part of this book may be reproduced or transmitted in any form by any means, electronic or mechanical, including photocopying and recording, or by any information storage and retrieval system, except as may be expressly permitted by the 1976 Copyright Act or the publisher. Requests for permission should be made in writing to: Bennett & Hastings Publishing, 7551 A 15th Avenue N.W., Seattle WA 98117, (206) 297-1991 or the address posted at www.bennetthastings.com.

Book and cover design by Jason Geiger and Geoff Gray

ISBN 978-1-934733-34-9

Dedication

I learned a great deal in writing this book.

Among the things I learned is the fundamental importance of having people in your life who believe in what's possible, and who support and encourage you consistently and relentlessly.

Terry Killinger has been a leader to me throughout this process, helping me keep my eyes on the vision and regularly daring me to make the leap.

It is said that to some degree we accomplish what the most important people in our lives believe we can accomplish. My wife, Paula Weiss, has always believed in me and in what is possible. Throughout our life together, and in particular during the growth of Path Forward, she has provided an abundant source of hopefulness and encouragement that has made all the difference.

This book itself is an example of what leadership can do in a person's life. Through Terry's and Paula's leadership I grew beyond myself and made a dream come true.

It is to them, and their leadership, that I dedicate *The Leadership Platform*.

Contents

Introduction 7

Self-Leadership 15

Plank 1: Make the Leadership Choice 17

Plank 2: Be Worthy of Followers 35

Plank 3: Cultivate Culture 51

Plank 4: Balance Thought and Action 67

Leadership of Others 85

Plank 5: Understand Motivation 87

Plank 6: Build Influence 105

Plank 7: Connect with Meaning 121

Plank 8: Leadership Language 137

Leadership of Teams 159

Plank 9: Create Shared Vision 163

Plank 10: Expect Accountability 179

Plank 11: Develop a Process View 195

Plank 12: Your Leadership Legacy 209

Appendix A: The Path Forward 360° Leadership Quality Assessment 225
Appendix B: The Path Forward Business Relationship Evaluator 233

About the Authors 236

Introduction

The Leadership Platform

Developing managers and leaders who create excellence in your organization

4 Balance Thought & Action	8 Leadership Language	12 Your Leadership Legacy
3 Cultivate Culture	7 Connect with Meaning	11 Develop a Process View
2 Be Worthy of Followers	6 Build Influence	10 Expect Accountability
1 Make the Leadership Choice	5 Understand Motivation	9 Create Shared Vision
—— Self ——	—— Others ——	—— Teams ——

Presenting the Leadership Platform

So you aspire to be a leader? Or perhaps you've been appointed to a leadership position, and you're not sure what to do next. On the other hand, you might be shying away from leadership – maybe you fear it's not worth the effort or the risk.

Scary, exciting, and confusing ... inspiring, overwhelming, and meaningful ... complicated, stupefying, and exhilarating – just a few descriptions of the experience of leadership. One word you won't find on that list is "easy."

No, you rarely hear a leader say, "I was fully prepared for the experience of leadership. I knew just what to expect. I had been educated and mentored throughout my personal and professional growth process, so I haven't made many mistakes, and I've never lost my head. Taking on the mantle of leadership was easy."

Yet more than ever, the world needs quality leaders, and for those who choose to respond to the call of leadership, somehow the difficulty and fear pale in comparison to the rewards reaped.

To paraphrase Shakespeare, "Some are born leaders, some achieve leadership, and some have leadership thrust upon them." Sometimes pure talent lands us in a leadership position. Sometimes it's a result of hard work. Sometimes we perceive a lack of leadership, and we step up and take charge. Sometimes a new position is created, and we just happen to be the best person available.

No matter how we get there, we usually aren't ready for our first leadership role – nor, for that matter, our second, or even our third. Each new role stretches us and makes new demands on our character, the quality of our thinking, our ability to connect with others, and our skill at developing the systems through which our organization does its work.

The Leadership Platform offers practical wisdom to make your leadership journey a little smoother and to increase the likelihood you'll succeed – and feel comfortable and confident doing so.

To be effective, a leader must stand on a strong, stable platform of attitudes, patterns of thought, intentions, and ways of understanding the complex world in which human beings interact. As a leader increases the scope of his responsibility and influence, he must continually build and remodel this platform, providing an ever-firmer foundation on which the weight of these responsibilities can rest.

Without this strong platform, the leader is at risk. Leadership is complex and challenging; a leader's platform must withstand multiple, shifting trials to her character, her intellect, and her ability to connect with and motivate others.

This book helps you understand the challenges of leadership as it guides you to build your Leadership Platform. It is not a detailed blueprint. It doesn't tell you the dimensions of each plank, the exact materials, or the cost or timing of the process. But it does offer a vision for the type of leader you could aspire to become as well as some tools to help get you there. The Leadership Platform also provides practical ways to monitor your own growth as a leader. We present this model as a way of breaking down a complex process into its parts – to make it easier to understand, to work toward, and ultimately to succeed at.

To the extent you are succeeding as a leader, it's probably because you've built a good platform. For you, the ideas in this book can help shore up your platform – refine it, make it stronger and more elegant. To the extent you're struggling as a leader, the Leadership Platform will help show you where you're vulnerable or incomplete.

Just as importantly, the Platform offers a model for developing other leaders. Ultimately, as you'll see, the most important role of competent leaders is to build organizations full of competent leaders. The Platform can help you select, coach, evaluate, and position people in your organization based on how their Platform is shaping up.

How do we build a Leadership Platform?

First of all, we build it patiently and persistently. We do it with respect for the complexity of leadership and the difficulty of learning it well. And we do it intentionally – we don't leave any of it to chance.

The Leadership Platform is a visual model – a metaphor – for the growth of a leader. We build it in three sections; each section contains four "planks." Each plank represents a set of ideas and beliefs, as well as a description of skills. As we lay each plank, we not only create a solid place to stand, but we also make room for increasing numbers of followers and fellow leaders to stand with us.

Your value as a leader is measured by the quality of the foundation you provide for those whose lives you influence – those whom you will help to recognize and attain their potential as individuals, as teams, as organizations.

The Platform's three sections

The Platform is built, to some degree, in sequence. While growth can occur in multiple areas simultaneously, we'd like to suggest that the building of each section depends, at least in part, on the sturdiness of the ones that precede it.

Leadership of Self. No leader can succeed until they've learned to lead themselves. As you lead yourself – as you develop a strong mind and character – you create a small but sturdy platform on which you can stand with confidence and make your mark in the world. In this section you'll learn that:

- to start building the platform, you must **choose leadership**.

- developing your character and growing your emotional intelligence skills will help you **attract followers** naturally.

- developing a positive and productive **culture** requires you to be an objective observer who reinforces the strengths and faces into the weaknesses of the environment in which you operate.

- leaders develop an enhanced capacity for **reflection**, rather than simply pushing their way through challenges.

Leadership of Others. Your ability to expand your platform depends on your ability to positively influence others in a one-on-one context. In this section you'll learn that:

- **motivating others** is a result of your ability to understand their needs and to connect them to the greater needs of the organization.

- leaders embrace the challenge and learn the skills of **creating positive influence** with others.

- your leadership effectiveness will expand as you **develop relationships** that focus on growth rather than just convenience or camaraderie.

- becoming an **effective communicator** creates clarity and incentive for others to excel.

Leadership of Teams. A new set of understandings and skills is brought into play as you learn how to lead complex teams of people and complex sets of projects and activities. In this section you'll learn that:

- teams will perform better for you if you facilitate the development of **shared vision** that pushes aside conflict and confusion.

- developing healthy **accountability** will insure that your team's standards and deadlines are consistently understood and consistently met.

- to build teams that perform, you must view work outputs as the result of **processes and systems**.

- your leadership capacity will blossom as you focus more on **your legacy** than on your importance in the moment.

Leadership development is a lifelong process, with infinite complexities. Here are just a few factors affecting the growth of a leader:

- how we were brought up – all the positive and negative beliefs and assumptions we've been taught

- our level of confidence in our own path

- the inherent complexity of human psychology, the chemistry of human interactions, and the strengths, weaknesses, and idiosyncrasies of those with whom we work and interact

- the ever-changing world of business, with its shifting markets, fickle stakeholder expectations, international politics, and subtle customer expectations

- the challenge of morals and ethics, of making tough calls, of accepting risk, of facing consequences

Again, leadership is not easy. Finding what may appear to be easy answers doesn't translate to good leadership; great leaders embrace complexity and challenge. Fortunately, for those who lead well, the rewards are astonishing.

Professional versus Personal Growth

Your personal goal to grow your leadership capacity should be separate from the goal of ascending the corporate hierarchy. Why?

A quick rise through the hierarchy can be deceptive. Young people have the opportunity to move more quickly through hierarchies than ever before. This is in part due to demographics: the dearth of experienced candidates often results in younger workers being promoted beyond the range of their capabilities. Leadership is largely a matter of maturity, so despite younger leaders' talent and hard work, they often aren't ready to take on the full range of challenges they've been given. So, while a promotion might imply that you've arrived as a leader, it doesn't prove you have.

There are damn few corner offices. Conversely, you also shouldn't view a failure to rise in the hierarchy as a failure of your leadership. Leadership is something that can, and should, be exercised at all levels of the organization. Organizations are flatter than they used to be. The more collaborative style of leadership in the 21st Century offers numerous opportunities to lead teams, projects, and interactions with customers and suppliers. Mature leaders see their positive impacts on the organization – the "results" of their work with and for others – as the true evidence of leadership. Your organization won't always be able to reward these results with promotions at the speed you'd like.

Why "climbing the ladder" is an ineffective metaphor

We often hear the term "climbing the corporate ladder" to describe a career progression. The ladder metaphor fails in several important ways. Here's why the platform metaphor works better to describe leadership growth:

- In climbing a ladder, the place you stand becomes progressively less stable. At the top of a ladder, it's difficult to get leverage. In building a platform, the place you stand becomes progressively more stable, so you can "lean into" your challenges with less and less fear.

- The ladder implies ascendancy; that is, to advance in your career, you must rise "above" the rest of us. On the platform, you stay at the same level as those you lead. The platform implies you stay well grounded as you grow.

- As you climb a ladder, you're at greater and greater risk of losing your balance and falling spectacularly. On the platform, you maintain balance, so your challenges and missteps are less catastrophic.

So I suggest you build a platform and forget about climbing the ladder. I don't know of many people who enjoy teetering at the top of a ladder. How much better to plant our feet on a firm foundation and work with confidence from there!

I invite you on a journey to build your leadership platform. In each chapter, you'll build a new plank. If you're open to growing, you'll find each plank makes you stronger and more capable – and thus more polished, self-confident, and appreciated by others.

Now, before we go any further – a warning. The Leadership Platform offers a compelling vision of an ideal leader. You will not measure up to the ideal attributes the platform describes – in fact, none of us ever builds the perfect platform. But as you'll learn, *it is the burden of visionaries to see the gap between what is and what can be*. If the Leadership Platform attunes you to that gap, it's doing its work.

Because when true leaders see the gap, they choose to get excited by possibilities rather than discouraged by reality. Leaders transform the painful realizations of today into aliveness – into the profound sense of satisfaction that comes from making things better tomorrow.

So why go to all the trouble of building a Leadership Platform? Why not enjoy life a little more – kick back, shed the stress? Why waste precious life energy when it might not make any difference in the end? Why not choose to feel good about ourselves without having to change? Why set ourselves up for possible failure?

For the leader, the answers to these questions are pretty simple. We don't know any other way to be in the world. We express ourselves through our leadership – our values, our beliefs, our fundamental hopes, our joy in engaging the world fully and courageously. And we know that our co-workers, our organizations, our communities, and our world are crying out for leadership – *aching* for leadership. If not us, who? If not now, when?

Those who provide leadership for others receive more than they ever imagined could be theirs.

Self Leadership

In the first section of the Leadership Platform, we will nail down four planks having to do with leadership of ourselves.

 Make the Leadership Choice (The Leap)

 Be Worthy of Followers (The Ripple Effect)

 Cultivate Culture (Put Down Roots)

 Balance Thought and Action (Boot and Sandal)

We start here because until you lead yourself effectively, you simply can't lead others.

Having said that, you can never fully master the first four planks. You can only move toward mastery – gradually, in fits and starts, and especially when life hands you difficulty or opportunity and the need for change stares you straight in the eyes. The growth of your leadership spirit, character, and rational thinking, along with control of your time and priorities, will always be challenges for you. Get help in this process. Keep reading, studying, and engaging with coaches and mentors, because this growth process is never complete.

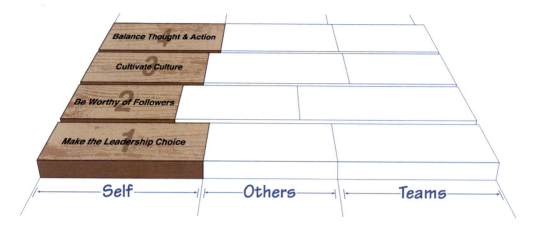

The foundation of leadership is in your intentions. The mechanics and skills are obviously critical, but many of us learn the mechanics without really examining our leadership intentions. You may wonder why this book deals so much with "fuzzy" concepts like "leadership intentions" rather than providing specific instruction in tactics. Two reasons:

- This book is about thinking like a leader and expanding your horizon to see the world on a broader and more conceptual scale. It's not about how to conduct a job interview, how to set up your calendar, how to provide performance feedback, or how to plan or manage a project. But after reading this book, you'll have the grounding to do these things well. The tactics will come much more easily to you when you're rooted in a leadership persona.

- There are many good ways to perform the tactical activities of leadership. For example, I've seen dozens of different ways to create and maintain a to-do list. But this book discusses why so many leaders fail to prioritize their activities – and that failure makes any to-do list virtually useless. The failure to set priorities is not a failure of technique, but a failure to understand what's important, and why. This book deals with what's important, and why.

It doesn't do any good to give someone a tool box and ask them to build a house if they don't have a picture in their head of what they're building and why they're building it – plus a strong intention to build it so it maintains its value and quality. With these intentions in place, we can then acquire the tools and build the house.

Plank 1

Make the Leadership Choice

Choosing to lead can allow you to make a difference in the world

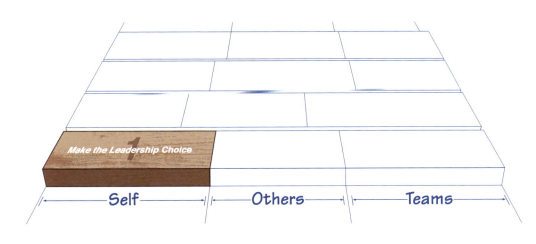

Having just celebrated his three-year anniversary at Bigbee Finance, Samuel is careful to "fit in." If he's a good soldier and does his work skillfully and dutifully, he thinks he'll eventually be rewarded with pay, with promotion, and with recognition.

Samuel sees some things that could be improved at Bigbee. He sees processes, strategies, and customer service policies he might change someday if he gets the chance to be in charge.

During lunches and breaks, Samuel hears his co-workers complaining about working conditions and management. He realizes more and more that Bigbee has a lot of work to do. The company is successful by most standards, but Samuel wonders how much more successful it could be. He stops short of bringing up any tough issues with his superiors, though. He doesn't want to rock the boat; he doesn't want to risk the next promotion or bonus.

Samuel goes home week after week, not particularly satisfied with his job, but not particularly dissatisfied either. When the Bigbee annual report comes in the mail, he only glances at it, assuming the financial numbers are beyond his ability to understand, or that it's all "just for the stock analysts" anyway. He asks no questions; he challenges nothing.

They look forward to the day they will be 'given' the opportunity to lead.

No one can argue that Samuel isn't good at what he does. He receives consistently good evaluations from his boss; he meets deadlines and performs his work error-free. But if you ask anyone at Bigbee what Samuel believes in, or what's important to him, or what his goals are, they wouldn't have an answer.

Samuel commiserates regularly with his friend Mike, who works for a distribution company. They both think they might need to change companies to find a place where their talents will be recognized and rewarded. They each look forward to the day they will be "given" the opportunity to lead.

But whether or not Samuel advances in his organization, he is not advancing in his capacity for leadership. At the core, Samuel believes he operates within a system created and maintained by others. Samuel is good at what he does, but he doesn't act on any ideas or dreams of his own. He operates well within the system, but he doesn't influence the system. He is unwilling to take the risks associated with being a change agent.

Samuel believes that leadership is something bestowed by the organization. He will be passive about what is going on around him until someone holds him directly accountable for change, or until the need for change has been spelled out for him by someone else. He believes he will need to be promoted and paid a higher salary in order to assert himself in a meaningful way as a leader. He prefers not to waste his energy trying to make things better at Bigbee. He believes the responsibility for change belongs to those higher up in the organization, those who are paid more than he is paid.

Samuel recently told his friend Mike, "When Bigbee promotes me – then they will see just how good I am."

Samuel hasn't made the leadership choice....

The Leap

There are many steps to building your Leadership Platform. Here's the first: making the choice to become a leader. It's not a simple choice – and it can change your life.

In a 2007 speech, Jim McNerney, President and CEO of Boeing, quoted his own father: "You have got to decide whether you want to lead or follow. That simple decision will go a long way to deciding what the rest of your career will be like." Until you've made this choice consciously, you'll be unable to build the rest of the Platform successfully.

It's a mistake to wait to be "knighted" – to wait until you're given the title, the authority, the *permission* to lead. Leadership isn't a position or a ranking. Leadership is a state of mind. To build your leadership platform, you must understand and embrace the mindset of leadership. It's really up to you.

For the observant leader, there is never a shortage of opportunities to lead. Leadership is needed at all levels of our lives: our friendships, our families, our non-profits, our communities, our government, and yes, our businesses. In fact, once you get into the mindset of leadership, you may find yourself overwhelmed by the opportunities you see. More than ever, the world needs leaders. Embrace the mindset of a leader, start developing the related skills, and you will be a rare and precious commodity.

What Hierarchy?

I once had an employee approach me, frustrated because he hadn't gotten the promotion he'd wanted. He asked, "How are you going to know what I'm capable of if you don't promote me?" But I already knew what he was capable of; and it was clear he hadn't yet made the leadership choice. He was waiting for me to give him a promotion in hopes he would lead effectively. No, thank you – I want to see people make the leadership choice before they're promoted.

In a healthy organization, you earn your position in the hierarchy according to your contribution to the health and success of the company. Whether you are a janitor or a junior executive, a barista or a board member, you'll start making contributions as soon as you start to think like a leader. You will be noticed, and promotions and pay raises will take care of themselves.

The choice to lead must be made repeatedly – daily – in big ways and small. Once you develop a sense of yourself as a leader, it becomes habit to continually ask yourself these kinds of questions:

- Is the circumstance I'm in calling out for my leadership?
- Am I willing and able to offer the kind of leadership that's needed?

The choice to lead can be as big as transforming an organization or as small as a thoughtful act of kindness; as big as recasting an entire business strategy or as small as apologizing to a client for a screw-up.

Why might you choose to become a leader? Well, that's different for different people.

Certainly there are bad reasons for wanting to be a leader. Maybe you're in it for the status or the money. Maybe you think achieving a leadership role might make someone admire or love you more. Maybe you lust after power, or you want to force your point of view on others. Part of the leadership choice involves doing a gut check with yourself about your intentions – weeding out some of these unwise reasons for seeking leadership.

There are, on the other hand, many wise reasons to make the leadership choice.

- Choosing to lead can provide you a powerful sense of accomplishment by giving you the opportunity to act on a larger stage and make a larger impact.

- Choosing to lead can be a way for you to "self-actualize" (in the words of psychologist Abraham Maslow) – to grow into your full potential as a human being.

- Choosing to lead can result in a fuller experience of life – the sense that "I gave it my all."

- Leadership can be fun. You can get the chance to work with great people toward meaningful goals. Achieving great things in collaboration is like a challenging game, with profound rewards for all the players.

- Choosing to lead can allow you to make a difference in the world. Many leaders perceive the needs of an organization, a community, or the planet, and are motivated by the question, "If not me, then who?"

Despite these rewards, most choose not to lead. Some reasons are obvious, others not.

- You might lack the self-confidence to lead.

- You might lack the energy or the drive. This can be situational; even the best leaders sometimes deem it wise to take a back seat.

- You might simply be risk-averse. In a society like the United States, where affluence abounds and most of us don't lack for basic needs, it's easy to get in the habit of protecting what we have rather than risking it in pursuit of something more.

- You might be operating in a high-risk environment, such as a culture that punishes dissent or open thinking, or an organization in crisis, so that just getting through the day is all you can hope for.

- You might be discouraged. Think about the word – dis-courage – and about the ways in which your courage might have been beaten down. You might have had a recent failure, or you might be surrounded by negative, dispiriting influences.

So to make the leadership choice, we must first assess our readiness to lead. There's no reason to criticize those who don't feel ready. It's just where they are.

But we can all agree that our organizations, communities, and the world could use more positive leadership. Think about the factors preventing you from making the leadership choice – in big ways and small – and ask yourself if you, and the world, might be better off if you made that choice.

The leadership choice is like facing the proverbial fork in the road. The "leaper" in the illustration on page 20 is someone who's taken a good, hard, honest look at the present state and decided it's incomplete, unsatisfactory – less than it might be. And though he's found that the road in the direction of leadership is not smoothly paved, he's decided to take a personal course of action, involving risk, to do something. The leap is an act of personal responsibility, of hope, of integrity, and of courage.

Leadership implies a restlessness – a consistent sense that the current state, no matter how comfortable, is not what it could be – and thus a consistent impulse to drive change. This restlessness is both a great burden and a great source of energy. The best leaders are "happy warriors": people who take joy in tackling the tough challenges.

Making It Real
The Choice to Lead

Describe a moment, or the moment, when you made your choice to lead. Tell the story behind your decision and explain the implications and effects of your choice. Often, articulating this to ourselves and others fuels our motivation to lead.

But to tackle those challenges – to be motivated to take the leadership leap – you also have to know what you're leaping toward. There's a gap in the illustration on page 20; the leaper must be clear about what's on the other side, and how compelling it is compared to the present state.

What's on the other side is the leaper's vision of what could be. Without a vision, there is no motivation for leadership. The challenge of leadership requires you not just to define that vision concretely, but to judiciously assess the gap between what is and what could be.

The Artist's Conception

Let's say you want to build a new deck in your back yard. What do you do? You draw up a set of plans that tells you the exact dimensions and the materials you'll use to build it. You may even draw what architects call an "artist's conception" – a drawing that translates the abstract concept of the deck in your mind into a concrete image.

What do you do with this image? You might show it to others, to get their support for the project. You might use it to convince your partner to help pay for it. Most importantly, you might post the image around the house to remind you how great the back yard will look when it's done. There may be challenges with the project, and some discouragements, so keeping the image of the deck in front of you gives you courage to make the leap and complete the job.

Your vision is a lot like the artist's conception. It has two important characteristics:

1. It's compelling and colorful enough to create the motivation to act.
2. It's concrete, tangible and specific enough to tell you when you've achieved it.

We've all seen the fatuous mission and vision statements that festoon the walls of organizations. Things like "We will strive ..." and "Through the commitments of our fabulous team ..." and "Customers are our first priority." What do they really say? What does "strive" mean? How do you measure "strive"? How would you know that your organization has truly made customers the "first priority"?

And why would I get excited about any of that? Show me the artist's conception! Make it beautiful, make it a "Wow!" Tell me how my life will be better if I follow you. Tell me how we'll know we've arrived.

In his wonderful book *The Fifth Discipline*, Peter Senge uses the example of John Kennedy's 1961 national call to action to land a man on the moon and return him safely to earth by the end of the 1960's. Kennedy was not a rocket scientist – he didn't know how to design an O-ring, or build a life support system, or plan a trajectory to a moving target a quarter million miles away. And many who did have the knowledge said it couldn't be done.

But Kennedy had faith in American know-how and in the power of vision, so he declared his total commitment to the project. "If we were to go only half way or reduce our sights in the face of difficulty," he said, "it would be better not to go at all."

And in fact, we did land a man on the moon – five months ahead of the deadline – and return him safely to earth. Even though Kennedy's life was tragically cut short six years before his vision was achieved, the vision was compelling and concrete enough to outlive him – to mobilize the American scientific establishment on the power of its momentum.

Do you have a vision? Would it pass the compelling and measurable tests? Say it out loud and ask yourself two questions.

1. Is my vision a compelling word-picture that describes a future I will be inspired to achieve, despite the risks and setbacks?

2. When the deadline arrives, will I know, without ambiguity, whether or not I've achieved it?

Why is it so important to be specific – to create a tangible vision? If we don't hold ourselves to this standard, we end up with fuzzy thinking about the future. The fuzzy thinking that plagues so many organizations is characterized by terms that describe unclear intentions, such as "want," "desire," "aspire to," and "seek," and useless comparatives like "more," "better," and "competitive."

One of the tests of your leadership will be to eliminate fuzzy goals and the fuzzy thinking that creates them. Fuzzy goals give you an out, because they can only be evaluated subjectively. If you say, for example, that you want to be "customer-focused," then you ought to have a way to measure that intention. Otherwise, if someone asks 100 people in your organization, "Is Bob customer-focused?" there would be no way to tell whose answers are correct. The only objective answer would be, "We have no way to measure that."

Making It Real
Vision for Yourself

First, complete the *Path Forward 360° Leadership Quality Assessment* (in Appendix A, page 225). Then, based on the results, draft a preliminary vision for your own development as a leader. Tinker with it until you can answer all the following questions "yes":

- Do you find it compelling? Does it motivate you to become a better leader?
- Is it a stretch for you?
- Is it concrete/specific?
- Is it timed (for example, "By November 30, I will ...")
- Is it measurable? (Decide what metrics you will use.)
- Is it realistic?

Once you've completed your draft vision, share it with others who can support you in achieving it. And keep it in front of you from now until the due date. Create action steps toward its realization.

The Gap

When we take an honest look at the present state and find it wanting, and when we develop a compelling artist's conception of the future, we're ready to confront the gap between what is and what could be.

Look again at the leaper in the illustration. Now imagine that the life of a leader *is* this leap. Your life, once you make the choice, will hang perpetually between what is and what can be. While living in this exciting moment, you appreciate everything you've accomplished and everything you have, and *at the same time* you desire a better place. It's possible – in fact it's *enlightened* – to be both perpetually accepting of the present state *and* perpetually pointed toward something better. This is one of the paradoxes of making the leadership choice.

Leaders are often troubled by what they see in the gap. Looking into the gap and facing the uncomfortable truths there can result in disappointment and frustration. Leaders turn this disappointment and frustration into action. Those who don't make the leadership choice turn their frustration into excuses for doing less than they can.

The leader studies the gap, no matter how complex and disturbing it might be. Change and growth can only be achieved if the gap is successfully leaped. This leap isn't an exercise in X-Games enthusiasm, but instead a thoughtful and considered action. We consider the width of the gap and we decide as rationally as we can whether or not we have the energy and the technique to leap it successfully.

This brings us to another paradox: *Leaders can never be 100% certain of success.* If you wait until you're entirely certain, you'll wait forever, and the critical moment will pass. As a rule of thumb, 80% certainty is the most we can hope for; in some cases we may have to leap when we're even less sure. *Making the leadership choice means being willing to leap without certainty of traversing the gap.*

And this of course brings up the "f" word: failure. You will have failures, and they will be public. As a leader, a healthy relationship with failure is critical. You must constantly walk a tightrope: you must learn to accept failure as part of the process of growth, but you can't be overly tolerant of it either. You can't be devastated by failure but you will certainly feel its sting. You can't be reckless, but you mustn't be passive.

Above all, you must mine failures for your learning, because for all the pain, they truly are opportunities. With your vision firmly in mind, you recognize the value of the journey. You'll learn to see setbacks for what they are: the explorations of a creative mind with a bias toward action and a guess about the future. Winston Churchill once defined leadership as "going from failure to failure without losing enthusiasm."

One last point about making the leap. As a leader, you'll make many leaps. In fact, as you get into the spirit of the leap, you'll learn the secret that leaders understand: the leap is where the *fun and growth of the journey* happens.

> **Making It Real**
> *Leaping the Gap*
>
> Consider a challenge in your workplace – a problem that affects the performance of the team, the profitability of the organization, or the motivation of the employees. This challenge must be one which you have not acted on in the past because you chose not to jump over "the gap." Discuss:
>
> - possible strategies for acting on this challenge in the future
> - the challenges and emotions you might experience in this process
> - the potential systemic and cultural barriers that might make change difficult
>
> Choose 1-3 action items you're committed to taking within the next 30 days to begin to address this challenge. Schedule these action items into your calendar.

Take-withs and Leave-behinds

To leap successfully, we must pack appropriately. And it's best to travel light – to take only what's essential to the journey. Too much baggage slows you down and increases the risk of delays and snafus – increases the risk that you'll fall into the gap.

What is packed in the leader's "carry-on"? Well, first of all, don't forget to pack your **vision**! When things get tough, it's easy to be tempted by detours, or even to forget why you undertook the journey in the first place. Keep your vision at hand, like the artist's conception, to remind you where you're headed, and why you took the risk.

Next, be sure to pack your **values**. Your vision should be in pursuit of your values, and your journey in harmony with your values. If you compromise these, whatever you achieve will not have been worth it. If you have to work to rationalize what you're doing, or if what you're doing just doesn't feel like the right fit, you'll never feel good about the journey, and you'll burn out before it's over.

The next category to pack is **encouraging influences**. Leadership requires courage, so you'll need to take along what *encourages* rather than *discourages* you. For example:

- Your will to succeed. Sometimes you have to look in the mirror and challenge the person you see there. Leaders don't quit easily; the best encouragement might well come from within – from your own sense of pride, your refusal to give up on the vision.

- Knowledge and education. Be a student of leadership. Your ongoing education, in whatever form, will give you fresh approaches and new skills. Sure, there are a lot of highly educated dolts out there, but outside education supported by hands-on experience is a winning combination. Grab as many opportunities to learn as you can, both inside and outside your organization.

- Your mental and physical health. If you don't feel good, either emotionally or physically, you'll wear out under the pressures of leadership. Take care of yourself and achieve work/life balance. A "whole" and balanced person is on a solid foundation and has the energy to contribute powerfully to the lives of others.

- Perhaps most importantly, you'll need to have the right people in your life. Spend time with people who energize and encourage you. Surround yourself with those who are invested in your success but won't shy away from challenging you. Find a mentor. Ask for help. Leaders don't hang with losers, cynics, or nay-sayers – they rob your energy and diminish your spirit. You'll need both to make the leap.

What should you leave behind?

You may need to leave behind some **old competencies** when you make the leadership choice.

Imagine you're an accomplished chef, and you decide to pursue restaurant management as a career. Your focus shifts from creating a great meal to creating a great dining experience. Surprise! *You can no longer cook the meals.* You've just given up part of your identity. You may be constantly tempted to go back to the kitchen, but if you do, you can't keep your eye on the total operation – and you'll alienate the fabulous chef you've just hired to help you succeed. *Nobody* likes being micromanaged.

This is quite often why leaders fail. Old competencies can be very hard to give up. Don't fall into this trap. Before you take your leadership leap, decide which skills will no longer serve you, and unpack them.

We talked about packing encouraging influences; make sure not to pack *discouraging* ones – bad habits, laziness, risk aversion, and relationships with people whose own failure to grow holds you back.

The choice to lead may put some of your relationships at risk. Closing the door on these relationships can be one of the most difficult steps on the leadership journey. You may find that some folks are uncomfortable with the journey. They may be afraid of change, or envious of your confidence. They may say, "Who the hell does she think she is?" You need followers who will accept your leadership, mature peers who don't see your success as a threat to them, and mentors who are invested in your future.

The culture of your organization may be too dysfunctional to support your journey. You might figure that your leadership leap will smack you into a wall, and thus you might want to change organizations. However, the world is full of people who think the organization is "the problem." Think hard about your contribution to the dysfunction before you seek greener pastures. You may find yourself playing out the same unsuccessful pattern in another position.

Take the time to reflect on the influences in your life and the personal and environmental factors that affect your ability to lead. A will to succeed, a hunger to learn, positive self-awareness, healthful habits, and associations with great people – these will get you as far as you want to go.

The Tension of the Journey

If you want a tension-free life, go live in a well-stocked cabin in the woods next to an idyllic stream. For the rest of us, tension is a way of life. In fact, confronting the gap between the current state and the vision *should* create tension. Dancer Martha Graham said this about artists, but she could have been talking about leaders: "No artist is pleased. There is only a queer, divine dissatisfaction – a blessed unrest – that keeps us marching." Or, in our metaphor, "leaping."

It's not the leader's job to eliminate tension in the workplace. Rather, it's the leader's job to create the right kind of creative, productive tension – and then to manage that tension well.

Music is an example of the transforming capacity of productive tension. The final chord of a piece of music resolves the harmonic tension deliberately created by the composer in the preceding bars. So there is tension built purposefully into most music that makes it emotionally satisfying for us in the end.

The physical properties of most musical instruments also employ tension to create appealing sound. The strings that vibrate in a piano or cello are under incredible tension. The air that flows through a saxophone is under controlled pressure. The surface of a drum is stretched tight to produce a pleasing resonance. In the same way, tension in the business world creates the possibility for members of an organization to make music together.

Take a guitar and pluck one of the strings. Gradually loosen that string by turning the key at the top of the neck while you continue strumming the string. You will hear the sound darken; quickly the string will become so loose that it no longer makes a musical sound. Now tighten the string back up until it makes the "right" sound. Tighten it too far, though, and it'll break.

Likewise, employees subjected to "destructive" tension will break if the tension is too severe or maintained for too long. The leader creates tension on the string, then constantly monitors and adjusts the tension to make sure it consistently plays the right "music."

If you exercise (and you should!), you understand that tension creates muscle growth. Sore muscles indicate the body has been put under stress; the body responds by strengthening those muscles. In much the same way, our leadership "muscles" become leaner and stronger when regularly challenged.

This need to create, monitor and adjust proper tension is as true of our relationship with ourselves as it is with others. Leaders too often turn up the tension on themselves to the breaking point, or allow circumstances or other people to do the same. Making the leadership choice requires us to understand that certain types of tension and certain amounts of tension are counterproductive.

> **Making It Real**
> *The Right Kind of Tension*
>
> Turn destructive tension into creative tension. Identify a situation, project, or initiative taking place in your sphere of influence around which some destructive tension currently exists. Describe the tension and name its sources. Determine the best options to overcome the tension, and then take action to implement a solution.

What distinguishes creative from destructive tension?

Destructive Tension	Creative Tension
You have no vision, or your vision is fuzzy, so you lack motivation.	Your vision is clear, focused and present, so your motivation is powerful.
You wish things would be better, but you're not taking action.	You take action to make things better.
You blame others for what's wrong. You believe you aren't accountable for changing it.	You consider your part in everything and take personal accountability when appropriate. You are less interested in who's at fault than in what can be learned and what can be done.
You are focused on safety; you stress comfort over achievement.	You see comfort and safety as signals of potential stagnation.
Your fear of bad things happening keeps you from taking risks.	You face your fears in pursuing your own potential.
You are isolated and uninformed, which further feeds your fear.	You have open lines of communication which enable you to understand present reality in service of your vision.
You aren't sure what's expected of you, and you don't clarify your expectations of others.	You work to create clear expectations and to live up to what's expected of you.
You aren't on the same page with those around you.	You communicate and connect with others in pursuit of common goals.
It's all about you.	It's about us.
Trust is lacking.	Trust flourishes.

When you make the leadership choice, you embrace change. Change creates tension. So when you make the leadership choice, you invite tension into your life. Without tension, there is no striving, no growth, no achievement. The key is to recognize the types of tension at work in your environment, and to maximize the creative and minimize the destructive.

Rationalization

As we've said, tension results from comparing the present state to the vision of the preferred future. One thing this "creative" tension creates is accountability – for yourself and others. Now that you've declared out loud what you intend to accomplish, somebody's likely to hold you to it.

Inevitably, though, you will at times fall short of achieving your vision. That's, of course, when you have to deal with failure.

Some might avoid setting specific and measurable goals – might shy away from accountability – to avoid failure. But a concrete vision, as we've seen, is powerful and motivating; and failures can be golden opportunities for learning. So the courageous leader, rather than worrying about his ego in the face of potential failure, does four things:

- forges goals in the fire of realism
- mines "failures" for their learning potential
- tells himself and others the truth about what has and hasn't been achieved
- moves on, minimizing guilt, shame, remorse, or self-recrimination

That third point about telling the truth points to a common form of rationalization – a way of "weaseling" on the leadership choice. Let's say I get tired of the peeling paint on my house. I pick out a beautiful shade of blue-gray and announce to family and friends I'm going to paint the house during my August vacation. Now it's September 23rd – and I've just finished the job.

I might ask myself the question: Did I fail? The house got painted, right? Wasn't that the goal? It was hard work, after all, and I did my best. It was hot in August, and the fishing was great. There were a lot of temptations. And it worked out great – the paint I used went on sale in early September, so I saved $100 by not buying it in August.

This is a shell game – a form of rationalization that narrows the gap by moving the vision closer to the present reality. In other words, you weasel on your vision, recasting it to make it appear you accomplished something you did not. This is dangerous if it becomes habit. Instead, tell the truth – face the reality that while the house did get painted, it didn't happen on the schedule you set. Is this a major disaster, a game breaker? Not necessarily. But next time the project might be bigger, the cost greater, the risk higher. Habitually giving yourself an "out" for falling short of your vision will be increasingly damaging as the scope of your leadership influence increases.

There's another damaging type of rationalization, as well – recasting the present state in a more selective light to make it appear closer to the vision.

What might that look like in the house-painting scenario? Maybe I proclaim that my funky house is just fine the way it is. The peeling paint is part of the ambience – the personality of the house. In fact, I've decided I like it better this way. Why go to all the trouble to paint? I'd be just like my neighbors; but if I leave it the way it is, I'll be special, unique, different.

There are many variations on the "I guess things weren't so bad after all" rationalization. Beware of this dangerous habit as well.

Leaders don't hide from their commitments, don't deceive themselves, and don't give themselves credit when they fail. But they don't beat the heck out of themselves for every failure, either. They learn from the experience and recommit to doing better next time.

Maybe the August date for painting the house *was* too aggressive. Maybe I didn't have the right tools. Maybe I didn't clear my calendar effectively enough. These factors were in my control. Or maybe it rained for the first two weeks of August, or I came down with the flu. These factors were out of my control. Either way, I failed to get the house painted during summer vacation. That's the truth. I intend to be honest about it, learn from it, and move on.

Plank 2

Be Worthy of Followers

I am accountable for my behavior
and for assessing the impact it has on others

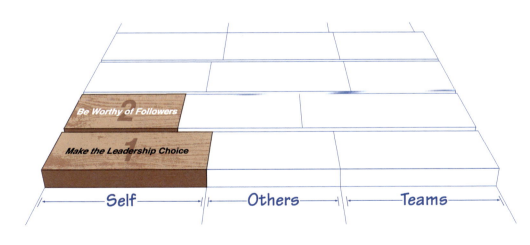

Ann was going places, and everyone knew it. She was the consummate performer – always ahead in her thinking, her work production, and her drive to succeed.

Ann entered the business world believing everything was a win-or-lose proposition. If she moved faster and fought harder than anyone else, she knew success would follow. If people got in her way, she'd just keep right on going. She had no time or energy for the "soft skills" she'd heard so much about. People issues were too much of a distraction for someone on the move.

Eight years into her career, Ann had advanced beyond most of her peers. She was managing a team of 12 on a $2 million implementation of a new accounting system. She knew there would be resistance to the new project; she'd prepared herself to "cut through the crap" and get it done. She refused to allow her project to be compromised by whiners and malcontents. Her team would either work to her expectations or pay the consequences.

Ann worked her team hard. Her interactions with them were limited to those issues that specifically affected the project. When her staff asked for meetings to discuss issues of importance to them, Ann responded, "We'll have time for meetings when the project is complete." After a few weeks, people stopped asking for her time.

Ann expected everyone to make the same commitment she did: total focus on the project.

She had no time or energy for the 'soft skills.'

One Monday, Tom, a member of Ann's team, called in to say he had to stay home to take care of a sick child. "But that's what baby-sitters are for!" Ann told him. "Your most important job is here."

Ann also had favorites. Of the 12 team members, three were trusted to work to her standards. These three got the bulk of Ann's attention and most of the desirable project tasks. The other nine were lucky to get as much as a nod from Ann in the hallway.

When something didn't go right on the project, everyone was sure to hear about it. Ann believed a climate of intimidation and fear was necessary to keep people motivated. She believed people would only work as hard, or do as well, as she demanded. Her temper was legendary. While this created a grudging acknowledgement of her passion for the work, it kept people at a distance.

Some of Ann's peers and superiors marveled at her energy and persistence. What they didn't see was the damage she was doing to the emotions, attitudes and motivation of her team. As long as the project was moving forward, Ann's peers and supervisors were happy.

All this changed on a fateful Friday. The project was about half finished when Dan, one of Ann's favored team members, gave two weeks notice. He told her he'd been offered a job at higher pay. What he didn't say was that he was not so much leaving the job as leaving Ann. While he respected her talent, he thought her a bad boss. He would never tell her that, but by leaving the company, he was silently "firing" her.

Ann got angry and frustrated. She was oblivious to the fact that she was the reason Dan was leaving. She sent a missive to the HR Director demanding the company salary guidelines be re-analyzed and raised for key positions "so we don't lose good people like Dan anymore."

In the weeks that followed, two more of Ann's people gave notice, both citing opportunities elsewhere. Even Ann, with her focus and her self-assuredness, had to step back and reflect on what was happening. She finally did an uncharacteristic thing – she asked one of her team members to help her understand why people were bailing. The employee blushed for a moment, then mustered the courage to say, "Ann, everyone respects your ability, but no one likes working for you."

Ann was speechless. Since she never made a habit of connecting with her team members, she was of course clueless about the animosity they felt toward her. She had seen her employees' emotions as "soft" issues; attention to those emotions was non-productive effort and time. For the first time, she began to wonder if all her talent and commitment might be wasted if she couldn't earn loyal followers.

She sought out her peer, Mike, who had an outstanding track record of performance but who also seemed popular and well-respected.

"Ann," he said, "my people react in powerful ways to how I manage my emotions and how I treat them. I don't see this focus on soft skills as a 'nice to have' – I see it as an imperative in a well-run business. And it starts with me. Unless I am emotionally mature and stable, and unless I understand the effect my emotions and values have on others, I will lose my followers and we won't get the job done over the long run."

The Ripple Effect

You added Plank 1 to your Leadership Platform by making a choice to lead. If you hammered that plank on straight, you now recognize that life will never be quite the same – you're an active, committed catalyst for growth and change. You've formed tangible visions of what the world might look like if your leadership aspirations are realized. You're ready to invite creative tension into your life and avoid destructive tension. You're ready to be honest about successes and failures, and to deal frankly with the realities of the present state, while maintaining hope and taking on risk.

Plank 2 is the next step in the process of putting your desire to lead into action. In Plank 2 you'll see that you must work hard on *yourself* to become the kind of person who is *worthy of followers*.

The Pond

Humans are intensely social. Every day, in the most obvious and the most subtle ways, we take thousands of clues from others about how we should feel about ourselves, the state of our organization, and the nature and flow of the relationships and interactions around us.

Imagine that your organization is a pond. Every action you take, every interaction you have, every gesture you make is a stone tossed into the pond, creating ripples that affect the people, systems, and processes around you.

Leaders toss larger rocks, creating bigger ripples. The more influential the leader, the more far-reaching the ripples. So to lead effectively, become aware of how you create ripples in your pond.

People respond at an elemental level to *who you are:* your character, habits, attitudes, and social presence. Their response to the personal qualities you possess – or lack – will determine to a large degree whether they will choose to follow you.

And this is the critical point: *followers choose leaders more than leaders choose followers.* The most effective leaders, quite simply, are those whose followers choose them. You might have *control* over the actions and circumstances of others. But if your goals are motivation, productivity and highly-functioning teams, control doesn't work in the long term.

It's the *impact* of your leadership that matters. Your leadership will be powerfully impactful when people around you find you admirable, trustworthy, and clear-headed enough to follow. As you grow your leadership platform, you will find that your followers are people you have *inspired* to act rather than *compelled* to act.

In fact, if you are a manager, and you're frustrated with the quality of your team a high turnover rate, it's likely that quality people are choosing not to work for you – or choosing not to work well for you. Of course employees look at other considerations – location, pay, benefits, and job responsibilities. But when these are roughly equal – and often even when they're not – the quality of leadership in an organization is the competitive differentiator that attracts quality people.

So the very first thing you do to put your leadership choice into action is take responsibility for the ripples you create. For 21st Century employees, the opportunity to work with respected, respectful leaders is an increasingly important consideration. If you act with integrity, purpose, and sensitivity, and if you strive to develop your character and your ability to interact effectively with others, you'll naturally have followers *whether or not you have institutional authority*. And as we saw in the last chapter, leadership doesn't depend on rank or title. Leadership is a quality of character, not a functional power derived from the blessing of an employer. You can be effective regardless of rank.

Making It Real
Your Pond Effect

Have an open dialog with someone who knows you well regarding your "pond effect." Invite them to provide frank feedback on what they observe in you. Journal the results of this dialog and how you felt about the discussion. Particularly discuss any "disconnects" between how you view yourself and how you might be seen by others, and discuss your reaction to this perception.

Showing up

Woody Allen once said, "Eighty percent of success is showing up." Nowhere is this truer than in the world of leadership. "Showing up" as a leader, with the right frame of mind and with the needed attributes, means you are ready to lead, and others will be drawn to you for the right reasons.

Just showing up as a leader can be hard work. Think of the thousands of interactions you'll have with others in the days and months ahead. In the morning you'll have to choose a parking space; even this is a form of interaction. Perhaps you'll hold the front door open for a fellow employee – or not. You'll walk to your desk or office a certain way – briskly or casually, smiling or frowning, greeting colleagues along the way or lost in your own thoughts. During the day you may attend meetings, eat in the lunch room, answer phone calls, give or receive feedback, work with a team to solve an immediate problem.

Throughout, you are making ripples in the pond, and the people around you will deduce clues from you about how things are going, how you're feeling, and whether or not you appreciate them, value them, even just notice them.

The effective leader embraces each of these interactions as an opportunity to create positive ripples in the pond. A good leader is constantly "mindful": constantly aware, focused and present to *this* interaction, and *this* one – assessing the impacts of her every behavior on those around her. It's not an easy, passive life. It's a life in which our intentions and our character are, well, obvious to most – starting with ourselves.

Leaders can't pretend for long, either. If your head isn't in the game, if you have harsh judgments about a peer or an employee, if you aren't supportive of a corporate directive – like it or not, it will show up in your body language, your tone of voice, and your demeanor. And because you throw large rocks into the pond, your negativity will damage the organization's spirit and will.

So face it: if you're a leader, you're on stage. Embrace the role; live it with spirit and integrity. If you don't want a starring role, there are important jobs backstage. But if you want to be a leader, get ready for the bright lights; get ready to live under the scrutiny of those you work with. This doesn't mean you needlessly draw attention to yourself. It means you are humbly mindful of the power you wield to change the course of a person's day, or even their life, by how you show up.

It might be tempting to dismiss much of this as the "soft" stuff. That's an antiquated notion. Virtually everyone who studies leadership today is clear on two points:

- What used to be called the "soft skills" are in fact what determines leadership success, far more than "hard skills" like expertise or technical competence. Leaders must practice the "soft skills" if they want to be productive, effective, decisive, and influential.

- As critical as they are, those "soft skills" are the hard skills to learn for most leaders.

My focus on soft skills is based on hard science. The evidence is now irrefutable that talent, intelligence, and even hard work are of little value unless they are matched with maturity, self-awareness, and an ability to maintain positive relationships with others. I refer you to the powerful, research-based work of Daniel Goleman in the field of "emotional intelligence." Running a business in which people typically have positive thoughts and emotions about their leaders is absolutely essential to the long-term success and profitability of the business.

Making It Real
Someone Who Inspires You

Write about a person in your life (not in your family) who has most "attracted" you as a follower. Tell which attributes most distinguish(ed) this person and attracted you to them. Tell how this person's influence stays with you today. Which of this person's qualities would you most like to emulate?

The qualities that attract followers

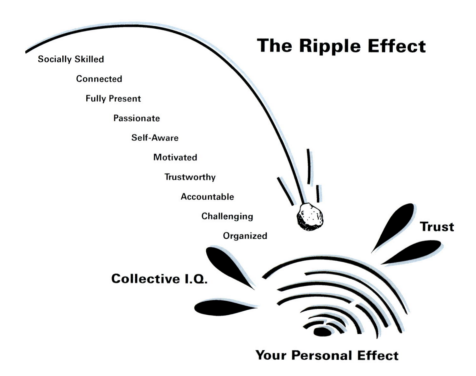

I propose ten qualities that will make you worthy of followers. These of course aren't the only ten; I encourage you to add to the list as you see fit.

1. Socially Skilled

Social graces are the lubricant for human interaction. They're the first quality we notice about others, and these first impressions often guide all our future judgments about people in powerful ways. Learn to shake hands firmly, make eye contact, use people's names, and say please and thank you. Return your phone calls, open doors for others, clean up after yourself, and don't take the last cup of coffee in the pot without brewing another.

It's amazing how much damage you can do if you're not mindful of the importance of social graces. It's amazing how much the presence of social graces adds to a leader's presence. Pay attention to these small "niceties" – they add up to a great deal.

2. Connected

You want your peers and managers to care about you as a human being, so if you want to be worthy of followers, extend this same gift to others.

Leaders make authentic connections with people they work with. In other words, they make appropriate attempts to get to know them as human beings – their interests, their values, their history, their aspirations. These connections serve several critical purposes.

First, they build the foundation of understanding and rapport that will support healthy communication, which is the lifeblood of any organization. To understand and be understood is of great value in the workplace, as it is in life. To be valued for one's unique personality, talents, and background is an even greater gift. When this understanding and appreciation come from a leader, it can be transforming.

Secondly, we motivate people best when we connect with them at a human level – and obviously the ability to motivate others is an essential skill for leadership. We'll discuss this further when we build Plank 5, on motivation

Building these personal connections takes time, and relationships are always complex, but true leaders recognize the power of well-formed relationships in the workplace. As a leader you must commit to forging and nurturing these authentic connections on a daily basis.

3. Fully Present

Too many of us are constantly, frenetically busy. We're victims of a dangerous mix of ever-increasing pressure to produce, plus technological tools that enable us to communicate with more people in less time than ever before. One byproduct of this ever-busy 21st Century work culture is the constant pull to multi-task at the expense of valuable interactions with others.

When you interact with a peer or employee, he or she should be the center of your universe in that moment. If you can't give someone your full attention, acknowledge it, apologize, and set another time for the conversation.

If people get the impression you're too busy for them, or that the next phone call or email is more important than they are, they will simply stop coming to you – and worse, likely resent you. This is no way to attract followers, and certainly no way to build your power and influence.

So when you're in a conversation or a meeting, the most important key on the cell phone is the one that turns it off. If you have the "pinging" feature that tells you a new email has arrived, turn it off unless you are a stock broker, a private investigator, or the National Security Advisor. The vast majority of us enhance our "availability" to others at the expense of our availability to the person in front of us – at the expense of our mindfulness in the here and now.

Being fully present also refers to your capacity to listen. Distractions don't just come from outside via phone calls and emails; your own thoughts can crowd out what is right in front of you. Listen with curiosity; listen for the purpose of understanding, rather than preparing your response (or planning your next meeting). More on this in Plank 8.

When you are with another human being in the workplace, your leadership presence is immediate, obvious, and powerful. Minimize distractions. Listen deeply and actively. Your colleagues need this from you – the realization that you take them seriously and you value them, their time, their thoughts, their concerns, their role in the organization.

4. Passionate

Organizations feed off their leaders' passions – for the company's values, products, customers, history, people, or achievements. What do you care deeply about? Is it obvious to those around you? Potential followers will want to know what you stand for, what's important to you.

Employees see this pretty simply. "Why would I care more about the company/customer/product than its leaders do?" One of the biggest rocks you throw in the pond is your passion for doing well, for beating the competition, and for running the best damn team, department, or company that you can. Know that passion is contagious.

You don't need to be a cheerleader or a charismatic speaker. There are many ways to show passion without engaging in public displays. You show your passion in the way you "show up," in the way you address the tough issues, and in your personal commitment to excellence.

5. Self-Aware

Leaders cultivate insight into their own strengths and weaknesses and commit to working with them to increase leadership effectiveness.

Being honest about your strengths and accomplishments, as well as your weaknesses and failures, is a sign of a confident, mature individual – as long as this acknowledgement doesn't spiral into either self-aggrandizement or self-doubt. Acknowledging our strengths isn't about bragging, and acknowledging our weaknesses isn't about making excuses – it's about our honest journey of growth as human beings.

The downside of being honest about a weakness is that we can use it as a crutch.

For example, I sometimes struggle with finishing things. I can be too much of a perfectionist. It has been easy at times to hold up this weakness as something insurmountable ("I'm just not a finisher"), implying that this character defect excuses me from completing a task or project. But with growing maturity and self-awareness, I now choose instead to learn better ways to manage my time and my task list. As a result, I've softened this tendency to the point where it doesn't have a significant impact on my life.

On the upside, acknowledging your limitations honestly opens you to others' coaching and support. I overcome my tendency not to finish things in part by seeking people who are more organized than I am. I appreciate people who have the courage to require me to set deadlines for accomplishing tasks and who then follow up on those tasks. People will help you "manage" your deficiencies if you acknowledge them and ask for help. If you don't acknowledge them, or if you rationalize them, you'll lose trust, and you'll get crucified for your weaknesses.

6. Motivated

Effective leaders find their own internal reasons for excelling and for working hard in the direction of their goals. They have a ready reservoir of personal motivation; they get the job done without prodding by others.

Because much of their motivation is "intrinsic" – derived from an inner source – these people are resilient when times are tough. They are not easily discouraged; they believe in their ability to come through any situation as a winner.

For obvious reasons, managers long for intrinsically motivated employees. But if you are truly intrinsically motivated in the workplace, you are in a small minority of the population. Why? Because although we're all intrinsically motivated in some areas (just think of all the things you love to do), in childhood this natural motivation tends to get driven out of us. In our culture, both education and parenting thrive on "extrinsic" motivation: incentives, rewards, consequences – "Do this, and you'll get that." We become dependent on rewards, expectations and approval from others. We become "other-directed" rather than "inner-directed."

Even if you've retained most of your intrinsic motivation, you're not likely to have an inexhaustible reserve of it. Even the most self-motivated leaders sometimes feel defeated by going it alone, by believing they can work their way solo through any challenge. Eventually almost everyone will wear out without the support and motivating influences of others.

You may be fortunate enough to lead a team of intrinsically motivated people at some point in your career. Maybe you can find – or breed – enough to fill an entire team or organization. But all of us need some extrinsic motivation, and some of us need a lot of it. In a perfect world, we would all work efficiently, exceeding expectations without any feedback from others. But then, we wouldn't be human, would we?

If there's a downside to being intrinsically motivated, it's the difficulty in understanding why others are not the same way. It can cause judgment and harshness toward those who require more extrinsic motivation. The better approach is to foster intrinsic motivation in others. We'll discuss this further in Plank 5.

7. Trustworthy

Let's not belabor the obvious: Without the trust of others, you will be unable to lead effectively. Trust is the foundation on which human relationships stand. Successful leaders consistently build this trust through their intentions and their actions.

We'll revisit this subject often as we build the Platform, but in general, being trustworthy means:

- following through on commitments
- being honest
- being willing to be held accountable
- being clear with expectations
- not seeking the expedient or easy path when doing right means taking a harder path
- maintaining confidences
- not being a hypocrite

Being trustworthy requires an extra level of energy and an extra emphasis on thinking things through. It requires a solid grounding in ethics and a keen awareness of the impact your behavior has on others. It means not cheating on your expense account. It means taking the heat when you've screwed up. Like all other aspects of leadership, you simply hold yourself to a higher standard. If you're unwilling or unable to do so, you won't succeed over the long run.

8. Accountable

Building on one aspect of trustworthiness (above), being worthy of followers means you are willing to be held accountable. Nothing will lose you respect faster than blaming others, blaming "circumstances," or spinning things in your favor when the going gets tough.

Here's a good rule of thumb for leaders: When something goes well, someone else did it, and when something goes poorly, it's your responsibility. Why take the blame and give the credit to others? Because leaders have faith they will advance their careers by producing good results and attracting followers – not by engaging in politically expedient behavior designed to make them look good.

You hold yourself accountable because it sends a message that it's safe for others to be honest with you. By acknowledging your culpability, you tell others that you see failure as an opportunity to learn, rather than to feel embarrassed, to rationalize, or to cover up. When you help others feel comfortable accepting accountability, you lift them out of a state of fear into a state of growth.

Too many young leaders are focused on being right and on winning. To grow as a leader, rid yourself of this tendency to see situations as either win or lose. Your job as a leader is to create as many wins as possible for as many people as possible. Do this by taking events past the finger-pointing stage. Point the finger at yourself – and then toward the future.

9. Challenging

Many of us remember that favorite teacher, coach, or boss who took us aside and told us, in the nicest way possible, that our performance was not up to our potential. While we may have found that experience uncomfortable, it was perhaps a pivotal point in our life. Without this challenge from a leader we looked up to, we might have continued to skate by – we might not have pushed ourselves as hard, we might not have put in that extra effort. We might not have realized we could do better until the first time excellence was expected from us.

Setting standards of excellence is hard to do consistently, in part because it takes skill to deliver the message in a positive, motivational way. Somehow it's easier to express disappointment or to compare people unfavorably to others. But the best leaders avoid these negative messages and simply challenge every individual to meet his or her highest potential.

When leaders see someone working at less than their best – whether it's an employee, a peer, or even a boss – they're troubled for a number of reasons.

First, leaders believe that a life worth living is worth living well – and living well means stretching and growing in sometimes difficult ways. When leaders see someone going through the motions, or crediting themselves for mediocre work, they are struck by the waste of human potential. As a leader, you are an evangelist for human potential – part of your mission is to shine a light on it, so others can explore it and fulfill it for themselves.

Leaders also challenge themselves and others because it makes work more fun, more meaningful, and more competitively useful. When people feel the thrill of accomplishment beyond what they thought they were capable of, amazing things happen – and they want to come back for more. People yearn to be in the presence of leaders who help create this experience with them.

10. Organized

Being organized might look like the "one thing that's not like the others" on this list. It's hardly a "soft skill," but its influence on potential followers is similar to other qualities on this list.

Being organized sends a message of respect for others. Being on time, being prepared, and following through on commitments in a timely fashion are all hallmarks of the organized leader – and all obviously help develop the trust we've identified as critical to attracting followers.

Conversely, disorganization is a form of disrespect to others – even if it's unintentional. Being disorganized implies you don't respect others' time and efforts. It indicates you are out of control. When you're out of control, you create uncertainty and doubt in others. People who can't rely on you won't perform for you.

Working with a disorganized boss or peer is a disheartening experience. It cheapens and degrades the organization. Being organized is not optional for leaders. We may chuckle about the piles of paper on our desk, or pass off lame excuses for not returning phone calls or responding to requests for information, but these actions clearly erode our ability to attract followers.

Making It Real
Ranking Your Attributes

Review the ten leadership attributes, and rank your strongest three and your weakest three. Discuss how you might gain greater productivity from your top three and how you might begin to work on those lowest three that represent the greatest barriers to your leadership potential.

Commit to a set of specific action items to make good on your intentions from this reflection. Share these action items with a trusted ally who can help keep you accountable.

Your Personal Impact

Nobody's perfect, of course – you'll never master all ten qualities above. But you can strive to exhibit them as consistently as possible, and in so doing you can create for others:

- an environment of mutual respect
- a high level of trust
- a deep sense of understanding and compassion between you and others
- a stronger "collective IQ," in which everyone is encouraged to be a creative planner and a problem-solver
- a workplace where people are eager to maximize their potential

If the stones you toss in the pond create these ripples in your organization, consider yourself a leader. You don't even have to be anyone's boss! These ripples can be your personal impact on the environment and organization. You will be noticed, appreciated, and looked up to by those who will quite naturally choose to be your followers.

Making It Real
The Power of a Role Model

Observe and comment on an example of positive leadership behavior exhibited in your presence, no matter where you observe it. Comment on how the approach the person used created a positive "personal effect" that helped resolve a problem or move a project forward. Discuss some of the other choices the person might have made and how the results might have been different had they taken a less productive approach.

Plank 3

Cultivate Culture

Be a student, an observer, a champion, and a critic of culture

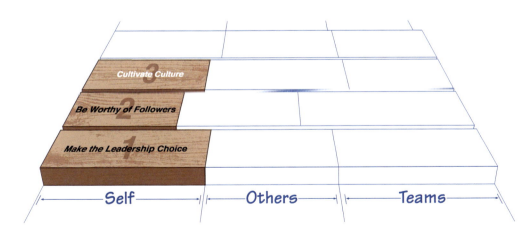

*E*ric had joined Brooks Products six months ago. Though only 32, he'd already logged some impressive experience. In eight years at Able Manufacturing, he had risen to the level of Marketing Manager.

In his first few months with Brooks, Eric's approach had been hopeful but tentative. He was happy to have landed with an industry leader. Brooks was known as a fast-paced company, and while they were about half the size of Able, their growth track had been impressive. But Eric's tentativeness was understandable – Able had laid Eric off unexpectedly just before Christmas last year.

Until the end, Eric had enjoyed working with Able. Their products were of impeccable quality, designed and manufactured to the strictest standards. Able never went to market with a product until John Able, the founder and President, was certain every conceivable customer requirement had been met, every design flaw eliminated – no matter how minor. The entire Able organization was visibly proud of the rarity of customer complaints and product returns.

Able's senior management consistently directed Eric to stress quality in their branding and marketing efforts. He'd learned to be cautious in pushing for early introduction of products. Able valued its zealous commitment to excellence over and above the opportunity to beat the competition to market. Quality was not to be sacrificed to speed. Eric was impressed by the company's 80-year track record and by the glowing testimonials he frequently heard from employees and customers. So he internalized the notion that devotion to quality was the key to the company's success.

And Able had been able to command a premium price for their products. Their customers knew they were getting something better – something worth the extra expense.

But during Eric's last 18 months with Able, the company's fortunes began to wane. Sales of their core product lines began to flatten; lower-priced (and lower-quality) competitors gained market share. Also, the paucity of new product introductions was beginning to erode enthusiasm on the part of end users as well as distributors. The company's reputation for quality was still intact, but the results weren't the same.

Culture develops and persists for a reason, and that's usually because at some point it was found that a particular approach worked.

The company's leadership, including Eric, held well-intentioned meetings to discuss the trend. Eric struggled along with everyone else to understand what had changed. John Able was especially frustrated. Winding down to retirement, he was not in the mood to be challenged with a crisis.

All the meetings yielded a single conclusion about the sales slump: a new generation of customers was simply not aware of the superiority of Able's products. Eric's marketing budget was boosted by 25%. He was instructed to emphasize quality at every turn. In addition, product engineers were told to build even more solid and dependable versions of the entire product line.

At the last meeting Eric attended at Able, John Able gave an impassioned review of the company's long history. He even dusted off the industry quality awards and passed them around to the management team. "Look at these awards," he said proudly. "This commitment to quality got us where we are today; the same commitment will get us through the slump." Reducing costs was clearly not an option; neither was finding faster ways to get new products to market.

Six months later, with the redoubled commitment to quality well underway, and with their new advertising campaign in full swing, the sales numbers had not improved. In the price vs. quality debate, customers were coming down on the side of price. They were also steering their purchases toward newer, more technologically advanced products. Something huge had shifted. The traditional, tightly held beliefs about quality no longer served Able well in these new market dynamics.

Eric was called into John Able's office. Thinking the company needed to be rescued from the brink of disaster, Eric mustered the courage to suggest, in the gentlest way possible – and among a number of other suggestions – that Able may have been over-engineering its products. Able might have to consider a fast-to-market approach, he proposed, reducing costs with creative, yet still ethical, shortcuts to the company's quality assurance processes.

Several days later, Eric was told his services were no longer needed. His superiors gave him glowing references and even helped fund his outplacement.

Unemployed for two months, Eric tried to sort out what had gone wrong. Able's products had retained their superiority, and Eric's marketing efforts had been crisp, stylish, and effective. But in the end, quality had not been enough, no matter how much Able believed in it. The company was so steeped in a culture of quality that its leaders couldn't objectively see what was happening. So even when the market stopped valuing the additional quality Able's products offered, the company couldn't respond effectively to the new challenges.

Hired on at Brooks, Eric found himself in a completely different environment. Brooks was an aggressive, take-no-prisoners sales organization. They didn't even make half the products they sold. They looked anywhere and everywhere for products their hard-charging sales force could turn around. Quality was important, but secondary. In fact, they took great pride in their ability to outsell competitors with clearly superior products.

Like Able, Brooks had an admirable track record. But now that Eric had had six months to learn, he saw some of the same warning signs he'd seen at Able. Sales were beginning to sag, and the company's response had been to do what it had always done – sell – harder, faster, more aggressively. Eric saw the exhausted looks on the faces of management as they exhorted the sales team with halftime speeches and promises of expensive vacations to those who exceeded their sales goals.

With the wisdom Eric had gained through his experience at Able, he could see clearly what was happening. The market had changed, but Brooks hadn't. Customers were finding other ways to get the products they needed. Also, new customer service capabilities and new technologies meant customers no longer needed to see a Brooks salesperson to resolve issues or fix problems with billing or delivery.

Once customers stopped relying on, and responding to, Brooks' sales techniques, the company was at a loss. Brooks' leadership – entirely composed of former sales people and sales managers – had made a faulty assumption. Since Eric was not yet steeped in Brooks' culture, he was able to see it with crystal clarity. Since the execs attributed the company's success to their aggressive sales approach, they assumed any failure of revenue performance was due to a failure of sales performance.

Eric knew other forces were at work. He was able, and willing, to extract himself from the company's history, beliefs, and assumptions to make a rational assessment about what was really going on.

Now the question became this: given how fervently Brooks believed in their ability to sell their way through any difficulty, was it possible for Eric – or anyone else – to challenge this thinking? Eric's wisdom and experience taught him not to get pulled down into stale thinking driven by a company's culture of previous success. But he also recognized how pervasive and controlling these beliefs can be. He felt intimidated by the challenge of driving change in a deeply-rooted culture.

Put Down Roots

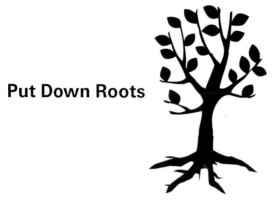

In Plank 2 in the Leadership Platform, we suggested your character and behavior make you "worthy of followers" – or not. We all yearn for an environment that validates us and encourages us to do our best.

In Plank 3, we discuss culture and values – how our thoughts and actions are guided, positively and negatively, by the patterns of thought, belief, intention and behavior of those around us. Like Plank 2, this plank proposes that every leader must be independently minded, aware of their impact on others, and able to spur themselves and others to higher, more productive levels of thinking. In Plank 2 we asked you to observe yourself. In Plank 3 we ask you to observe the world around you and to break through into a place of rational, creative thought. This place is reached only through understanding where we come from, where we've landed, and how both individuals and organizations root themselves in systems of belief that can serve them well – or kill them off.

Let's use the example of a tree. A tree is a magnificent combination of strength, beauty, and durability. It can survive wide variances of weather and continues to grow all its life, providing shelter to humans and habitat for countless other creatures. The roots of the tree plunge deep into the ground, seeking nutrients – creating a system that can be a third or more of the total weight of the tree. The system of roots, which can't be seen, is just as much a part of the tree as the visible trunk, branches and leaves above.

The roots of the tree serve essential purposes for the tree, keeping it alive under sometimes challenging circumstances. But the root system also presents tremendous obstacles to its survival. Once rooted, the tree can no longer move – if external conditions change, the tree cannot find a more suitable location!

The tree's root system resembles the culture of a business. From its culture, the organization can derive its strength and sustenance. However, like the hidden root system, an organization's sometimes-invisible culture can make the organization – or its leaders – immobile.

Perhaps the best description of "culture" is that it defines the way people within it understand and experience the world socially. Culture encompasses everything from our language to our religion, our food, our legal systems, our dress, our moral precepts, the way we share wealth and resources, and the way we assign different roles in society based on age, gender, and education.

When you become part of an organization, you become part of its culture. As a leader, you must strive not to be swallowed up by that culture, but instead become a rational and unbiased observer of it. You must become aware of how the culture impacts your thinking and belief system. You must become aware of the various ways a company's culture drives its strategies, actions, and attitudes.

Ultimately, as a leader, you help to establish and enforce the culture. These ways of thinking and understanding the world are largely driven from the top, and then taught to succeeding generations of employees. If culture is ever to change, leaders must change it.

Eric's story illustrates two companies with starkly drawn cultural boundaries. The first company's culture is driven by an obsessive focus on quality. In that culture, those who believe in and produce quality are rewarded. And since one aspect of culture is that it tends to punish or discourage "outsiders" with different norms, negative consequences accrue to those who question or attack Able's quality orientation.

Think about all the ways a culture becomes embedded – in us and in our organizations. Culture guides our decisions about everything – whom to hire, whom to sell to, how relationships are structured, whether or not to expand, how to respond to challenge. And as long as success is achieved, the culture gets reinforced – it's seen as "correct." Said differently, as long as positive conditions exist, the tree will grow its roots deeper and deeper into the ground.

Culture develops and persists for a reason – usually because at some point it was found that a particular approach worked. For example, Americans are a very hard-working culture. Hard work is in part what has led to our status as a superpower. Similarly, many other aspects of personal, organizational, and societal culture have a positive and legitimate basis in the real world.

Culture also provides us with a richly shared set of experiences. It breeds comfort because it provides an environment where most people think and act like we do. We seek this in our businesses as well as in our communities.

Here's the problem: because of its deep roots, culture is resistant to change – especially when that change threatens the norms of the culture itself. So when externalities change – as in the case of both Brooks Products and Able Manufacturing – the company's culture can hinder its ability to adapt. Like the tree, a fortunate culture might find itself in a place where it can flourish without having to undergo radical change. But for most of us, and for most organizations and societies, change occurs so often that the culture must remain adaptable if it is to survive.

The role of leadership is to develop and champion a positive, productive, and consistent culture. But there is a paradox. When the organization faces difficult change, the leader must be able to objectively determine which aspects of the current culture will serve the company well in the future, and which will not. Perhaps the biggest challenge of leadership, therefore, is to observe the intersection of culture and conditions, and to drive themselves and their organizations to adapt.

Every organization is a complex organism in which a variety of cultural influences are at play. Of course, cultural variations are endless, but let's discuss a few common examples:

A "work-hard play-hard" culture. People are expected to work long hours and to participate in "team-building" activities outside of work. This culture might create strong bonds of mutual regard and interdependence, but it will cheat its members of work-life balance.

A "smart" culture. People are rewarded for the quality of their intellectual contribution. This organization may achieve at high levels in an innovative and technical arena, but its high-IQ leaders might be bored by the day-to-day requirements of running the business.

An entrepreneurial culture. The motto here is, "Every dollar is an opportunity to make two." This organization is always on the lookout for a great investment or to pioneer a new product or service. It's an exciting group; members enjoy putting themselves and their money at risk in the hopes of making much more money in return. If you're risk-averse or prefer a stable work environment, you might not fit well here. This organization succeeds and fails spectacularly. It's better at starting a new business than at managing it once it's up and running.

A culture of harmony. Healthy relationships and conflict resolution are valued highly. Decisions are reached (if they're reached at all) through a process designed to satisfy as many different people and perspectives as possible. Everyone is listened to and honored. This highly collaborative approach can be great for morale and works well in many cases. But the focus on harmony can paralyze the organization, preventing it from moving forward until everyone agrees on the ideal course of action.

Every type of culture has certain characteristics:

- Decisions are driven by the beliefs and assumptions that arise from the cultural "way of knowing."

- People who don't embrace the culture feel like outsiders.

- The organization builds around its culture to such a degree that real change is often hard to create.

Keep in mind that you also have your own personal culture, so the above characteristics also apply to your personal journey: your decisions and actions are driven by your personal "way of knowing." You probably have a hard time connecting with people who are different from you, and you likely find it hard to change even when external conditions seem to demand it.

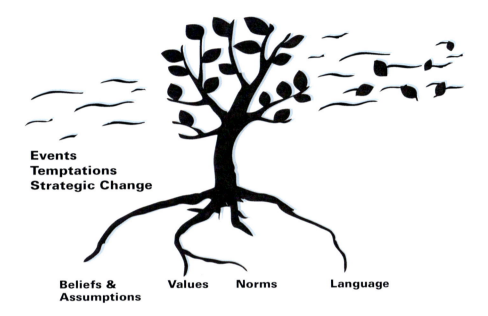

The Roots Of Culture

What is culture made of?

Three components of culture largely define the cultural "roots" of you and your organization. Though not the only three roots, they are likely to play an important part in your leadership career. Remember, as an insider, you need to be able to step out of the culture and study its components objectively and dispassionately so as not to become too "rooted" in them yourself. You need to respect the strength and permanency of culture while moving aggressively and thoughtfully to change it when change is needed.

1. Values

It's become common – perhaps fashionable – for organizations to create a Values Statement or other public document that might include declarations like these:

- We will exhibit integrity in everything we do.

- We will be a welcoming place in which all our employees feel valued.

- We will strive to do our very best in all areas of our business.

- We will focus on the customer and do everything necessary to insure their complete satisfaction.

- We will share openly with our employees, customers and suppliers any issue which affects them.

Clearly values are important. In a world in which tremendous wealth can be generated – ethically or not – many companies try to stay grounded by reminding themselves of what's most important. Stating values out loud and reminding people regularly can create accountability and guide people to "do the right thing." But there's a danger to publicly stating your values: you will now be judged by others on the alignment of your actions with those values.

What is a value? In one sense, it's the worth of something as measured by what we're willing to exchange for it. In other words, when confronted with two or more options, our values are revealed in the choice we make. If we own a 1965 Mustang, and someone offers us a 1964 Corvette in straight exchange, we'll soon find out which car we value the most. Likewise, when given a choice between an action that reflects integrity and one which gains us status, power, sex, or money, we'll soon find out how strongly we value integrity.

Values are also reinforced by our organization and our society. In some societies the rule of law is valued more than individual liberties. In other societies, religion is the highest value; in still others, great focus is put on the environment, or on the arts. The historical culture of our families, institutions, and businesses greatly influences how we spend our time and our money – a clear reflection of our values. One could argue that the primary role of government is to sort through conflicting cultural values and to support those values held most closely by the largest number of people – or to forge compromises so these diverse cultural forces can coexist peacefully and productively.

A value can also be seen as something having an intrinsic worth beyond money – something worth doing or having for its own sake. Hard work is a good example. So is integrity. Even when they don't produce anything of real importance, hard work and integrity are seen by many as having high cultural merit. These values may not be tangible, but they make us feel good about ourselves.

Values are an important cultural "root" – perhaps the most important root of all. Without strong values, we can drift and make bad choices. But leaders must be serious about values – if you claim integrity as a core value, you have to really mean it. As a leader, you will be held to a higher standard. If your behavior is inconsistent with your stated values, you erode trust; if you violate your values to get ahead, you won't be a leader for long.

2. Beliefs and Assumptions

A belief is "the conviction of the truth or reality of a thing, based on grounds insufficient to afford positive knowledge." So by definition, if you act from a belief, you aren't working with conclusive data.

An assumption is defined as the "act of taking for granted, or supposing." So acting on an assumption means taking into account even less data than acting on a belief.

Making decisions based on beliefs and assumptions is essentially guessing. Now, these guesses can be highly educated, based on years of experience and a reasonable calculation of risk. If 'A' has always led to 'B' in the past, it's reasonable to assume 'A' will lead to 'B' once again. But if the 'A' action doesn't get the 'B' result the next time, the leader who isn't aware of his underlying beliefs and assumptions may not understand why history didn't repeat itself.

A strong culture leads to strongly held beliefs and assumptions. These can be both useful and dangerous. Let's use the example of Brooks Products. In Brooks' culture, selling was the core competency – the predominant way of interacting with the world. All of Brooks' challenges were seen as sales challenges. A certain set of beliefs and assumptions underlay this thinking.

First of all, Brooks believed that customers responded first and foremost to a great sales effort. Yet there was only minimal evidence to support this. Brooks did have positive sales growth and performance over a course of years. But the connection between the performance of their sales force and the sales results they achieved was not established by empirical evidence. Brooks saw the results and assumed their sales force's behavior was responsible. They never tested that assumption by trying different approaches to customers to see if the results changed.

A great deal of our thinking forms along these lines. We see an outcome; we look for events or conditions that occur concurrently with that outcome; and we draw a causal connection. Right or wrong, that connection becomes a belief or an assumption that guides future behavior. It's a classic logical fallacy: the fact that 'B' follows 'A' does not necessarily mean that 'A' caused 'B.'

Of course, not all beliefs and assumptions are wrong. But when they are right, it's often due to luck and the law of averages.

The role of leadership is very important here. When we embrace a belief, we desperately want it to be true – otherwise, our ego is challenged. To protect our ego – individual or collective – we sometimes twist reality in a way that reinforces rather than challenges our belief. When Able Manufacturing experienced a persistent sales slump, the company's leaders wanted it to be an issue of quality, because quality was what they believed in. When it turned out not to be a quality issue, they resisted challenging their core belief – they resisted developing an understanding that would have led them to a more fruitful course of action. To admit that quality was no longer valued by the market would have meant that their culture and belief system were somehow wrong.

In the best interests of any organization, its leaders must respectfully challenge all its beliefs and assumptions, testing their validity and their efficacy in dealing with today's problems.

3. Norms

Norms are an organization's lived rules of behavior – written or unwritten. They are the "dotted lines" outside of which your actions might get you in trouble. It's interesting how powerfully norms can control behavior without ever being explicitly stated.

For a rule to qualify as a norm, most members of the organization must conform to it most of the time, and there must be consequences (formal or not) for violating it.

Punctuality is a good example. Regardless of whether it's ever been written down or verbalized, if the leader shows up on time and expects everyone else to do the same, employees are likely to adopt that norm. But in most organizations (by my observation) punctuality is not enforced. Even if there's a written rule about showing up on time, punctuality is not a norm if it's typical for people to violate it, and if there are no consequences for doing so. It is helpful to establish written guidelines for behavior, but they're not norms unless they're enforced.

Another example of a norm: permission to speak uncomfortable truths to authority – or not. If people feel punished for speaking these truths, they will stop doing so and it will become a norm to withhold them. "Thou shalt not speak truth to authority" is unlikely to be a published norm, but rather a learned behavior with clear consequences, and therefore a norm.

Great customer service is another example. Through consistent example, and through reinforcement by leadership, it can become a "rule" in an organization to jump through hoops in the pursuit of customer satisfaction without the rule ever having to be written down or publicized.

People quickly learn the norms of their workplace. They do so by observing which behaviors are accepted and which are shunned.

4. Language

Of the roots of the cultural tree, language is the one whose powerful impact – on our thoughts, motivations and behavior – is hardest to grasp. Why? Because our very *thoughts* are made of words. So trying to see the impact of language on how we think – our values, beliefs, and decisions – is like trying to fix the wheels on a moving train.

What is reality for each of us anyway? It's not what we *perceive* – that's just data. Your reality is how you *interpret* what you perceive – the meaning you make out of it. It takes *language* to give meaning to our perceptions.

Words paint experience in particular colors. The colors we use influence how others around us see, interpret, and make meaning of our experiences. The language we share as a company culture shapes how we view reality together, and thus how we think and act.

For example, when a company's values conflict with each other – say a "just-git-'er-done" attitude conflicting with a value of open and honest communication, or a strictly regimented management hierarchy conflicting with an emphasis on creativity – the way the conflict is *languaged* with employees profoundly influences how they'll choose to behave.

How the word "failure" is defined and used can be another example of the power of language in shaping the culture. Does the culture encourage leadership risk-taking and talk about failure as learning opportunity? Or does it tend in its communication to punish those who don't meet goals?

We'll revisit the concept of "leadership language" in a different way in Plank 8. For now, tune into how language is used in your team or your organizational culture. Notice how it differs from how it's used in other arenas of your life. Become a student of the effect that language has on how people think and act. Stay awake to possibilities of more effective uses of language.

Windy Weather

Let's take the tree analogy a little further. As they do with trees, windstorms can test the strength of an organization and its root system. These storms can take the form of temptations and events.

Temptations – often about creating a short-term win at the expense of an organization's values or culture – can wear many guises. For example:

- fudging the truth about one's products to increase sales
- using inside information inappropriately
- procuring a big contract by offering an "incentive" or "gift" (a.k.a. bribe) for the purchasing agent.

If the roots are strong, though, the winds of temptation will not damage the organizational "tree."

Events can also threaten the root system. For example:

- a new competitor moves in and begins undercutting prices
- the economy slows down, causing sales to do the same
- an executive with key industry relationships passes away or retires unexpectedly
- the consumer safety folks label one of your products unsafe and pull it off the shelves

Whether event or temptation, the bottom line of the windstorm is the bottom line of the company: money. When the company is under financial duress, it's easy to drift from values and norms that have served the company well during the good times. Remember, you are what you do every day. It's easy to forget who you are when times get tough.

Again, values are the "tap root" of the individual and the organization. Even in the face of significant strategic winds, the organization must adhere unwaveringly to its values – or consciously, transparently change them. Otherwise, employees and other stakeholders will feel betrayed.

The most difficult event-related wind to stand up to is the wind of fundamental strategic change. Examples:

- technology changing the interaction between you and your customers
- restructuring, expansion, or acquisition
- fundamental changes in products or services
- changes in skill sets required for a large percentage of employees
- automation
- changes in sales strategy
- fundamental changes or pressures on compensation models

When these types of events occur, the "rootedness" of the organization into a particular way of thinking or being may become a fatal deficit rather than a strength. Again, as a leader, you must be willing to assess your own culture and that of your organization. Are you approaching the new challenge with a clear head, unfettered by the beliefs, assumptions, and norms that served you well during a different time or circumstance?

As a leader, you must be able to ask these questions:

- How is our culture serving us now?

- Are we trying to relive the past or are we developing new ways of thinking?

- Can we continue to thrive using current beliefs, assumptions and norms?

- If not, what will it take to shift them?

Making It Real
Understand Your Team's Culture

Based upon what you have read in Plank 3, explore the following:

- To what extent is our organizational culture sustaining us?

- What defines our culture? What are its hallmarks?

- What's working for us in our culture? What's not working? Think about these components:
    - Values
    - Beliefs
    - Norms of behavior
    - Language

- What external influences are coming toward us? And how will our culture adapt?

- How does my team's culture – as a subset of the larger organization – play into all of the above? What's working? What needs to be changed?

- Based on these reflections, what are the next leadership leaps for me?

- What specific action steps am I willing to commit to in the near future? When do I intend to undertake them?

The paradox of the cultural equation is this: that which roots us powerfully can also immobilize us. The failure of many leaders and the failure of many organizations is a failure of adaptation. Said more simply: things changed – but we didn't.

Leaders are passionate about their beliefs and about the strengths of their organizations, but they are also capable of being dispassionate observers, willing to challenge every assumption and every belief in the pursuit of success, however they define it. They seek out diverse points of view to counteract the narrowing of perspective that tends to plague organizations over time.

The leader engages in clear thinking – including awareness of, and empathy for, the challenges that change brings. Remember how dearly we hold onto our beliefs and how threatened we can feel when those beliefs are challenged or proven wrong. Leaders don't put their organization at risk in the interests of protecting old and useless cultural roots, but neither do they act recklessly in changing that culture.

When the leadership challenge becomes one of changing hearts and minds, the leader has to decide whether doing so is feasible, and whether it's worth the time, effort, and risk – and changing culture almost always demands time, effort, and risk. However, in too many organizations, leaders stand on the sideline. They know change needs to occur but they're unwilling to tackle the tough issues. The defining moment of your career may come when you see that this deep "root-level" change needs to be made, either in yourself or your organization, and you choose whether to step up to the challenge. This moment requires you to be a student, an observer, a champion, and a critic of culture.

Plank 4

Balance Thought and Action

My intentions are the intentions of a leader, and I spend my time accordingly

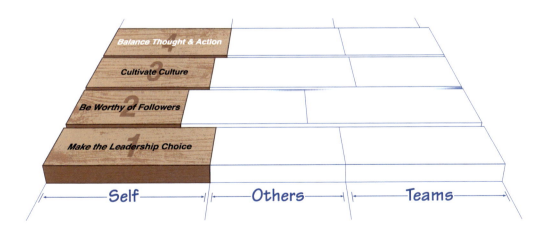

Adam had just been named "Employee of the Year" at Sensol Manufacturing.

A day-shift supervisor in the manufacturing plant, Adam was admired for his quick intelligence, his strong work ethic, and his fairness to all employees. His team appreciated that when they needed an answer, he was always there with the right one.

Each morning, Adam grabbed the production planning documents and headed to the floor to make sure the day's quotas were met. These varied a bit – sometimes there was a rush order, occasionally a more efficient piece of equipment would boost productivity for the long term – but all in all, the quotas were pretty consistent. Adam had earned the nickname "Hundred-Unit Harry" for his team's ability to produce 100 units on nearly every shift.

Each day, dozens of little challenges came up and dozens were resolved. Adam moved quickly from one issue, one conversation, and one task to the next.

Adam loved his job. He'd worked for Sensol for seven years and still left the plant nearly every day with the satisfaction of a job well done. A good manager, Adam had learned, was a guy who knew his stuff, who rolled up his sleeves and got busy, who overcame the day-to-day challenges through sheer force of will and the ability to "work the system." Sometimes the methods Adam used weren't all that… graceful. He carried a hammer on his tool belt, and at times he found that balky equipment responded to a little "encouragement" from it.

Adam's team had high morale. They enjoyed the consistent achievement of the 100-unit goal – it united them, gave them a sense of camaraderie. Led by Adam's good example, they would do "whatever it took," including staying late, pitching in when others needed help, or taking up the slack when a teammate was sick or on vacation.

> "You're the glue that keeps the team together. We can't risk having you off the floor working on strategic planning."

Several months after Adam received his "Employee of the Year" award at the annual banquet, he was called from the floor to attend a meeting with the other plant supervisors. Even the night shift folks had been called in, so Adam knew something was up. Sure enough, the company's VP of Operations walked into the room and delivered a startling message.

The company's #1 customer had received a lower bid from Sensol's biggest competitor. Unless Sensol could respond, it would lose the account – with devastating consequences. The bid was almost 20% less than what Sensol had been charging. "Obviously," the VP said, "our only recourse is to boost our production rates by 20% – without increasing costs."

Adam was a bit stunned – he'd have to figure out a way to produce 120 units a day.

He decided to call on his trademark "winning attitude" and take a positive approach with his team. Calling them together for a brief stand-up meeting, he shared the news and asked them all to make a commitment to the new production goal. He hinted at serious consequences if the goals weren't met and told them he'd do everything in his power to help them. For the most part, though, Adam stayed positive. He pictured himself as the motivational coach in the locker room, exhorting his team to give "120%" to win the game in the second half.

Every day over the next few weeks, Adam's team met the new production quota. To do so, he canceled all training sessions and assigned maintenance staff to the production line two to three hours a day. Performance reviews piled up, but no one asked Adam to explain. He kept smiling, kept working hard, kept giving 120%. Adam felt more important and more valued than ever before.

Then problems began stacking up. Adam's patience started to erode, and he noticed his frustrations growing. He started noticing how many things were left undone at the end of his shift. He watched equipment efficiency decline, and he noticed small quality issues slipping through the cracks. These things annoyed him, but he didn't have time to deal with them – his team needed every hand on the production line.

After achieving the 120-unit goal every day for almost a month, a glitch in the supply chain resulted in a one-day production of only 92 units. There was nothing Adam could have done to prevent the shortage. Arriving early the next morning, Adam picked up the production schedule and noted incredulously that his shift was expected to produce 148 units to make up for the previous day's shortfall.

Adam marched into the plant manager's office, flashed the production schedule and opened with a volley. "We've never come close to 148 units in one shift!"

The plant manager looked at him and smiled. "Adam, you're the man. You've always figured out a way. I have confidence you'll meet this goal."

Adam returned to the plant floor and took a quick walk to blow off steam. As the employees started filing in, he told each of them they were going to need to "kick ass to get 148 units out the door" that day.

An hour later, one of the two production lines was down – a conveyor belt had broken. No one knew whether a replacement part was available. The one person who knew how to repair the conveyor was out that day, and because trainings had been postponed, no one had been cross-trained to fix it.

Adam had been concerned about this conveyor for months but hadn't had time to research alternatives or entertain bids. The plant manager had told him to look into it, but this issue had taken a back seat to the urgent short-term production requirements.

A few weeks earlier, the line foreman had suggested that the conveyor system could be eliminated altogether with some tweaking of the production line. Adam was intrigued. He had set a time with the foreman to discuss the idea, but twice emergencies had come up, and the brainstorming session had been postponed.

Still hopeful of hitting the magic number 148, Adam mobilized a fire line of employees to grab the products at one end of the defective conveyor line and carry them one by one to the other end. Meanwhile, he tried to figure out how to patch up the conveyor until it could be fixed. He even took a few swings of his hammer. He only succeeded in denting the equipment and making a lot of noise.

Shortly after lunch, he and the line supervisor took stock of the situation. The employees on the fire line were exhausted. And they were only falling further and further behind the production goal.

Adam's line supervisor grabbed him by the shoulders. "This company is asking too much of you," he said. "You've always done what they asked, but this is just crazy."

Adam looked down at his sweat-stained shirt and felt the soreness in his head and his hands. He took a look around and breathed a heavy sigh. "I guess there's just no way we'll work our way through this one." He felt the burden of defeat.

The next day Adam noticed his plant manager in conference with some of his peers. They were drawing rough diagrams of new plant layouts. Flip chart pages taped to the wall were labeled "Training," "Processes," "Equipment Upgrades," and "Cost Reductions."

As he attended to his usual duties on the floor, Adam wondered about what he'd seen. Later, he found an excuse to pass by the plant manager's office. He poked his head in and asked, "How did the meeting go this morning?"

The plant manager looked up at him. "It went pretty well, but we have a lot of work to do."

"How can I help?" Adam asked.

"You can do what you've always done," the plant manager said. "Keep things together out there on the floor while we address these longer-term issues. You're the glue that keeps the team together. We can't risk having you off the floor working on strategic planning."

For a moment, Adam was proud of being "the glue." But as he walked away, he wondered how proud he should be. What would result from this strategic planning? After years of being a good soldier, what would be his future role? He walked to his office, sat down heavily, and plopped his feet on the desk. As he gazed absently at his well-worn work boots, he felt a sense of powerlessness, and for the first time, a strong concern about his future at Sensol.

Boot & Sandal

On our leadership journey so far, we've made the choice to lead (Plank 1), we've determined the importance of character in attracting followers (Plank 2), and we've considered the influence of culture – patterns of values, beliefs and norms – in shaping how we and our organizations think and deal with change (Plank 3).

Now we get to the matter of how we spend our time. And "spend" is the operative word here, because time is your most important – and ultimately, in the metaphysical sense, your only – asset. Face it: when you're gone, the measure of your life will be how you spent your time.

Your growing platform needs another plank. To nail it in, you must acknowledge the tension between your tactical or everyday activities, and the need to step out of the flow so you can plan, organize, and develop. For the majority of managers, the tactical easily wins this battle: the urgent, as someone once said, is always getting in the way of the important. But the successful leader balances what needs to be done today with what needs to be done to prepare for tomorrow.

We depict these two aspects of our work with a pair of images: *the boot,* representing the active work of today, and *the sandal,* representing the reflective work that engages our higher thinking in pursuit of our vision for tomorrow.

My intentions are the intentions of a leader, and I spend my time accordingly.

This implies you have to take the time to create intentions. So what are the intentions of a leader? Well, they're not just to survive or to process the next transaction. The intentions of a *manager* are to insure the successful day-to-day operation of the enterprise. The intentions of a *leader* are out there – over the horizon – in the future.

If your intentions are those of a leader, you'll have to spend time in "sandal" activities:

- *Planning and Strategizing:* Making sure your organization's position in the marketplace (or in the larger organization) stays viable, flexible, dynamic, and resilient, and offers opportunities for growth.

- *Analyzing:* Looking for trends and information that give you an overview of what's going on beyond today's transactions.

- *Studying:* Increasing your capacity, and the capacity of others, to do more effective work and produce greater outcomes.

- *Relationship Building:* Reaching out to develop a network of people who can help achieve the vision.

- *Developing:* Teaching, coaching, and mentoring, as well as designing and implementing training and development systems that insure the consistent nurturance of quality employees and other leaders.

- *Communicating:* Framing and delivering the visionary messages, clarifying direction, keeping people focused on the long term, and articulating compelling reasons for others to do their best.

All these activities lead us to big-picture thinking – a hallmark of effective leaders. *Where are we going? What do I need to know to chart a course? What's happening now that informs our journey? Who will accompany me on this journey? How will I communicate where we're headed and how to get there? How do I enrich, encourage, and stimulate my team to make a positive impact on their lives and the lives of others?*

Look carefully at the bulleted list above. Did you spend any appreciable time on these activities this month? This week? This afternoon? If you're like most business people, you probably spent precious little time on them. Instead, your time was likely spent on administrative trivia, deadlines, and putting out fires.

No one, not even the most senior executive, gets to spend her entire day on "sandal" activities. But every job above entry level should be a combination of both types of work.

Examples of boot activities, or active work

- taking customer calls
- answering questions or giving short-term guidance
- composing emails and making phone calls on logistical issues
- conducting tactical meetings
- driving, moving products, cleaning, organizing – physical work
- completing repetitive paperwork: invoices, compliance documents, filing, etc.
- gathering price quotes and conducting routine sales work

Examples of sandal activities, or reflective work

- engaging in an off-site long-range planning session
- reading a business-related book, article, or trade magazine
- taking a business-related course or seminar
- analyzing metrics or financial reports and looking for trends and patterns
- dialoguing about planning or strategic issues
- observing and inquiring into the work of others; seeking ways to improve operations
- developing new processes and training systems
- writing performance reviews, coaching, mentoring

Reviewing the lists above, most of us would say, "It would be nice to get more time for reflection, but there's just too much to get done." We understand the value of sandal work but we tend not to spend much time doing it. Why? Let's start with the least obvious, most controversial reason – we may not really want to *do* the sandal work.

American business culture biases us strongly toward action. How often have you heard some variation of the phrase "just git-'er-done"? It's ingrained in us that success is a function of how hard we work and how badly we "want it." In many organizations, people are rewarded for doing what I call "heroic" work: stubbornly plowing ahead, boots a-blazin', to meet the needs of customers, bosses and co-workers despite all obstacles.

Truth be told, we often enjoy being the hero: that knowledgeable, experienced, capable person who, despite all obstacles, leaps a tall building in a single bound to get the work done. Remember Adam, the character in our opening story? He tried to expand output solely through commitment and hard work, and when it worked, he felt valued.

Active work is quite simply more seductive than reflective work – especially for "working managers" who have a lot of tactical responsibilities. Why?

Active work provides immediate gratification. At the end of the day, you look back with satisfaction to a stack of papers processed, a quota of products produced, or a list of phone calls made. Even though the work may be physically taxing, require a lot of time or energy, and involve challenges, seeing the results feels good – the same way it feels good to have finished washing the dishes, changing the oil, or balancing the checkbook.

Reflective work, on the other hand, offers delayed gratification at best. People promoted to positions requiring more reflective work often complain about leaving work feeling like they didn't accomplish anything. They may, in fact, have accomplished a great deal, but the payoff for their work might not come for weeks, months, or even years.

The pursuit of immediate gratification – doing what's expedient and pleasurable instead of what really needs to be done – is an epidemic in our culture. It underlies not just our work habits, but many destructive personal and societal habits as well. The choice between dashing off a few emails and completing that overdue performance evaluation isn't so different from deciding between ice cream and fresh carrots, or between exercise and a hot bath. Dealing with delayed gratification requires patience, intellectual discipline, and a big-picture focus.

Active work is also appealing because it typically involves the use of previously acquired skills or knowledge – work we already know how to do, work we feel competent doing. When we reflect, plan, or strategize, on the other hand, we're creating new pathways of thought, which involves a steep learning curve. Climbing that learning curve isn't always fun.

For the above reasons, reflective work is in many ways harder than active work. There's a physiological component to this as well. Have you ever wondered why you're so exhausted after an all-day meeting? ("I didn't do a thing; I just sat there. Why am I so tired?") The brain consumes an enormous percentage of the body's energy and oxygen when it's learning something new or pondering something complex. At some level, we are taking this into account when we're avoiding a challenging cognitive activity.

Ironically, despite all of this, many of us simply don't see reflective work as "work." My clients often wrap up coaching sessions or strategic planning meetings by saying, "Okay, now I need to get back to work." This betrays a prejudice against reflective work. Many of us feel guilty if we aren't engaged in short-term, tactical activities. Leaders who come up through the ranks often feel disloyal to their hard-working line employees if they spend an afternoon in planning or analysis. It's too easy in our culture to equate activity with effectiveness. Yet how many of us would call Chicken Little "effective"?

So maybe you've been deluding yourself. Maybe you've been putting off important reflective work not because you truly don't have time for it, but because deep down you know it involves a taxing level of concentration, challenge and effort that you would rather not muster. Carving out time to do the important, long-range reflective work is thus a matter of hard choices and discipline. It's more than just trying to cut through the usual "busyness." It's about resisting the strong cultural and personal bias and the habits that draw us toward active work. As a leader you must recognize these dynamics and acknowledge this very important fact:

If you wait until you have time to do the reflective work, it will never get done. The amount of active work waiting to be done will always expand (with your passive acceptance and assistance) to fill the available time.

Why is it so important to balance boot and sandal work?

Like our friend Adam, the leader who does not balance thought and action is doomed to rely on heroism – continually trying to force his way through problems rather than thinking his way into opportunities for growth.

When you're wearing your work boots, you're operating in experience mode. While you may be quite competent in this mode, you risk becoming stale – failing to grow.

When you're wearing your sandals, you're operating in learning mode, or growth mode. This is where you have your greatest impact as a leader. It's where you tap your deep well of creativity, where you foster dynamic growth. It's what leads you ultimately to outperform your competition.

If you're not in balance – if the vast majority of your work is active, "boot" work – you may be a significant tactical contributor, but you won't elevate your team or organization to the next level.

And you won't elevate *yourself* to the next level either. By being the "hero," Adam got labeled by his superiors as a doer and not a thinker. When the time came to solve the systemic problems, he was left out of the loop. He had excluded himself from the higher levels of problem solving by being essential as a "boot" worker.

The organization was unwilling to pull him from the manufacturing floor because he had perpetuated a system in which heroic individual behavior was necessary to the day-to-day operation.

I'm not trying to paint an unrealistic picture here. I'm not suggesting you can always find a quiet place to retreat to where you do nothing but think and create. What's more important – and more practical – is seeing boot work and sandal work as concurrent.

Every day we're confronted with problems to solve. Do you solve them temporarily or permanently? When you solve them temporarily, you probably provide a solution based on your experience – or by simply doing the "boot" work yourself. Of course many problems do require immediate action. But in the process of solving each problem, do you explore whether it has a deeper cause – a more systemic source – and do you plan to take "sandal" action on *that*? Do you offer someone a fish, or do you teach someone how to fish?

When we segregate boot and sandal work, we fail to engage consistently with critical long-term issues. Management retreats are great, but they only happen once in a while. The best leaders do the work while they ponder how to do it better.

So how do we begin to think like the best leaders?

- *Prioritize* sandal activities in concrete ways. Schedule time for them weekly, if not daily. (We'll offer strategies later in the chapter.) Don't wait until they're convenient for others, or until the rare window opens up between events. Have the courage to put boot activities aside for the sake of a longer view – the leader's view.

- *Define* the benefits of specific reflective work carefully to yourself and others. If you feel that taking a particular class or engaging in a team-building activity is important, cite the impact you expect it to have on you and your team. This can help justify the time spent and get the support of others to make that time available.

- *Sustain* the effort over the time required. Most sandal activities are not one-time efforts.

- *Delegate* your boot work to others – never as easy as it sounds. More about this, too, later in the chapter.

- *Use a coaching approach,* whenever possible. When you are overseeing or participating in tactical activity, question whether you are coaching or directing. Directing others to complete work is a boot activity. Coaching is simultaneously a boot and sandal activity – achieving immediate outcomes (boot) while offering people tools to solve problems on their own (sandal).

- *Offer questions instead of answers.* A leader who has all the answers is not growing and not helping others grow. And a leader who thinks he has all the answers is deluding himself for the sake of his own unhealthy ego.

- *Imagine!* In Plank 1, we talked about leaders as visionaries – people who regularly look over the horizon and live in the world of possibilities. If you're content to live in the day-to-day status quo – to exist in work-boot mode all the time – you aren't thinking like a leader. If you are thinking like a leader, you'll find the constant pull of tactical work to be a barrier to your broader ambitions. Exercise your visionary capacities. That's sandal work.

Becoming a Process Thinker

We'll talk more in Plank 11 ("Develop a Process View") about the role of process thinking in the leader's mind, but let's give it a little preview here.

The work that an organization accomplishes is the result of processes that have been established to do the work. These processes may be inconsistent from department to department, they may be poorly defined and documented, and they may not be well measured or managed. But there is a process to all work, good or bad.

I've found one of the hallmarks of effective leaders is the habit of seeing this connection – that all work outputs are the result of the quality of the processes employed to produce them. If you can learn to see all the tactical occurrences that consume your time as *outputs of processes*, then you'll become more oriented toward fixing processes than toward fixing immediate problems.

Making It Real
Overcoming Process Interia

Look hard for a process directly within your sphere of influence that you have followed and never questioned to this point. Focusing on all the direct and indirect influences and on why that process is handled the way it's handled, ask "what if?"

See if you can, by engaging your reflective mind, find a way to accomplish the work that would quantifiably improve performance and productivity. Document the details, estimate the time and/or financial benefit that might be achieved, and share the proposed new process and the expected benefits with your team. Then modify the approach as needed based on the team's input.

When a time sensitive event such as a production snafu, a botched order, or even the sudden departure of an employee occurs, the process-oriented leader looks to solve not only the short-term cause of the problem (the machine broke down), but also considers the possible systemic issues related to the event (we have yet to establish a dependable routine maintenance procedure) and finds time to work on that as well.

In the end, process limitations led to Adam's downfall, defeating even his best intentions and his hardest work.

Strategies for sandal time management

The barriers to creative, progressive, proactive thinking are not only the psychological ones described above. They're systemic and institutional as well. So a big part of the challenge is *time management*. Remember that your intentions are the intentions of a leader and you spend your time accordingly. So let's discuss some practical ideas for creating a balance between thought and action.

1. Use a prioritized to-do list every day.

    - It continues to surprise me how many managers fail to maintain this discipline (perhaps because it's a sandal discipline!). Sadly, it explains how a lot of managers approach their work – reactively, rather than proactively. In other words, constantly playing defense rather than offense. To not work from a prioritized to-do list implies you don't see your time as intentional – that you actually expect to get swept along by events.

    - While many managers do keep to-do lists, not many prioritize them – which also leads to reactivity. If your goal is to simply get things done and cross them off, you're not being intentional enough with your time. Use a simple priority A, B, or C classification.

    - Your to-do list should include dates for all your activities. Don't list them all for today! A to-do list can be intimidating and demoralizing because it reminds us how many things are not yet done. Dating the activities can reduce stress by putting out of your mind those items that can wait until tomorrow, or next week, or even next year.

    - Now that you've got an effectively prioritized list (and congratulations for taking the sandal time to maintain your list!), look at the things to which you've assigned high priority. How many of them are sandal activities? How many reflect the intentions of a leader? Or are they all tactical, work-boot activities?

2. Keep a disciplined calendar.

    - Prioritizing your to-do list and including sandal items is a great start – and it's not enough. Keep a calendar and block time for sandal activities on it. Again, I'm surprised how many managers try to work through their day without a good calendar discipline. This is especially dangerous in shared-calendar environments such as Microsoft Outlook®, where others can schedule your time. If you haven't proactively blocked out time to learn, strategize, or develop, you will find your time hijacked by less important meetings and activities. You won't be spending your time with the intentions of a leader.

    - Many managers spend the regular work-day in survival mode, reserving sandal activities for evenings or weekends. Certainly projects requiring deep reflection are best undertaken when things are "quiet." But it's too easy to fall into the pattern of avoiding all sandal time during the work day. Once you're in this habit, it's difficult to break it.

3. Extend your planning calendar.

    - Do you schedule activities more than a few days or weeks into the future? If you extend your planning calendar several months out – and perhaps even a year or more – you'll be less likely to get trapped in the tactical world, and more likely to stay focused on sandal activities.

4. Use your action bias to divide larger projects into smaller tasks.

    - It's daunting to see an entry on your to-do list that says "complete performance reviews" – when ten of them need to be done, and each review has six steps. Better to list ten different reviews with ten different dates, and schedule time for each of the steps. This breaks down the larger task, making it less intimidating and increasing the likelihood you'll get a good feeling from at least getting started.

    - Project management can help here too. Sometimes a large project, such as training your staff on a new procedure, deserves a separate project planning document. But the individual tasks from that larger project may want to get transferred to your to-do list – such as "secure a meeting room," or "complete training module #1," or "finalize training personnel list and distribute announcement for first class."

    - What we're talking about here is deceptively simple. You'll feel like you're solving problems, but you're simultaneously moving the organization forward strategically, step by tactical step.

5. Turn your wish lists into actionable plans.

    - Most of us find ourselves saying "someday," or "when I get time." We know in our hearts this often means "never." So when you find yourself using "wishing language," turn that language into actionable plans and steps. Nothing is more demoralizing than compiling a mental list of goals and then regretting that you never got around to taking action on any of them. After all, as we noted in Plank 2, one characteristic that makes you "follower-worthy" is following through on your commitments – even those you make to yourself. Otherwise you're out of integrity. And the leader who loses integrity loses followers. Talk is cheap; if you create intentions, make good on them.

6. Delegate tasks not appropriate for your level.

    - Failure to delegate keeps us in boot mode. Five reasons for not delegating have direct implication for the boot/sandal balance:

        a. We fail to delegate because we've failed to hire, develop, and train quality employees.

        b. We fail to delegate because we've failed to produce documented and repeatable processes for our employees.

        c. We fail to delegate because we've failed to provide our employees with the equipment or technology they need.

        d. We fail to delegate because we're too emotionally invested in our role as "doers" and "heroes." We secretly don't want to offload work because it may take away our sense of accomplishment – our pride in being the "go-to person."

        e. We fail to delegate because it would free us to face the sandal work, which we're avoiding because it's... harder.

    - The first three above are failures of the system, but the system becomes less efficient when managers are overbalanced with boot activities. An insidious reinforcing loop occurs: you don't delegate because you haven't taken the time to train employees or develop processes or upgrade equipment; as a result you perform more and more heroic work and spend less and less time fixing these systemic issues that drove the work back to you in the first place.

    - Here's a simple way to evaluate how well you're delegating, as well as how well the system supports the work that needs doing. List the tasks you currently perform in one of the following three columns:

Only I Can Perfom	Others Could Do	Others Could Do if properly trained or if the system were modified

- If you are honest in producing this table, you'll probably see that you could delegate much more than you do, and that the system is driving work back up the hierarchy.

- A good rule of thumb is that all work should be given to the lowest level employee capable of performing that work efficiently. This means not only are you running a lean organization, but lower-level employees are being challenged with opportunities to learn and apply new skills.

Making It Real
How Do You Spend Your Time?

Keep a diary of your activities for a full week, then slot each of the activities into one of the three columns in the form above. Journal the implications for needed delegation and training. Also discuss ways in which external influences *and* your own internal habits, inclinations, fears, desires, comfort level, etc. may be keeping you in "fire-fighting" mode, or keeping you from optimally delegating.

Commit to a small number of action steps for the coming weeks in order to implement some of your ideas. Schedule these action items into your calendar.

Achieving a balance between boot and sandal – between action and reflection, between strategic and tactical – is one of the most consequential challenges facing a leader.

It takes courage to recognize that when we get trapped in tactical mode, the trap is often of our own making. It takes patience, persistence, vision, and time to lead the charge for systemic change when necessary. But the alternative – staying in inefficient tactical mode – is the most vicious of vicious cycles. The result can threaten the competitiveness, and thus the very survival, of any business.

Extraordinary will and mental discipline are required to keep your sandals on despite the urgency and attraction of boot activities. If you believe you can work your way to success, you're only partly right. It depends on what you call work. It depends on how much time you spend on activities linked to planning, learning and development for you and your team.

Making It Real
Understanding Your Role as a Leader

Rewrite your job description. Don't describe what you do, but rather describe the critical strategic objectives your position is or should be accountable for achieving.

Then do a thorough comparison between what you tactically do in an average week and what your strategic job description should call for.

Finally, make a plan for transitioning some of your regular activities so that they become more aligned with your strategic job description.

Leadership of Others

With courage, and in the knowledge that we will always be a work in progress, let's move on from the Leadership of Self section of our Platform to the Leadership of Others section. Four planks comprise it:

 Understand Motivation (Buried Treasure)

 Build Influence (Earth and Moon)

 Connect with Meaning (Eye Contact)

 Leadership Language (Turn on the Lights)

In these four planks, we'll discuss your intentions for building powerful, positive, and growth-generating relationships.

In 100 years, your business probably won't be around. The product or service you sell will probably disappear, or transform into something very different. What will remain in 100 years is the legacy of the impact you had on others.

Relationships in the business world are full of richness, complexity, challenge, conflict, and nuance. The leader who leaps into these relationships with courage, care, and positive intentions will find his work more than half done as a result. One by one, the leader reaches out and creates relationships that are honest, that probe the depths of understanding, that explore the heights of mutual accomplishment, and that create growth for everyone involved.

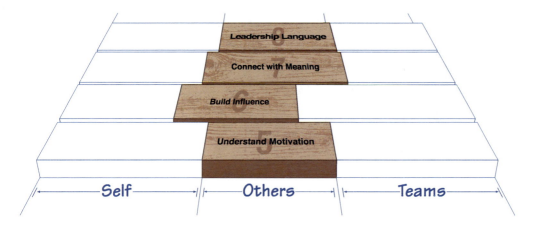

These relationships will of course help you get your work done; but more importantly, they will generate most of the joy and satisfaction of leadership. Let's explore how to create relationships of value, and thus continue to build your leadership intentions, understanding, and character.

Plank 5

Understand Motivation

I create a motivating environment to maximize performance and results

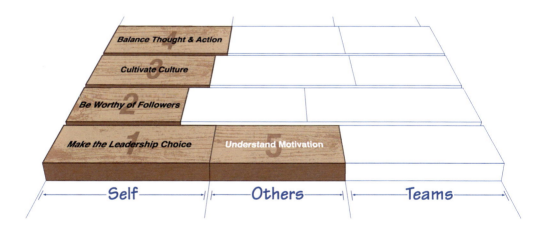

Bob was always trying to get his employees to do better work. He'd heard all the tricks about how to reward employees with cash bonuses, extra time off, and even the occasional gift of food or gift certificates to the local mall. He used these tools diligently.

Bob was also big on accountability. He set goals and measured results, he publicly reviewed performance, and he stressed the importance of an efficient and productive department. He also made sure people knew when they fell short of his expectations.

When things didn't go right, Bob would make sure the error was acknowledged. He would document employee performance problems in writing, following to the letter the "progressive discipline procedure" established by HR. He was far from abusive or impatient – in fact, he would always speak in a soft and understanding way. He would bring the offending employee into his office, patiently explain the problem, and ask for the employee's attention to the matter in the future.

Bob considered himself tough but fair. This combination, he'd heard, would always do the trick.

But these strategies didn't seem to work as well as he'd hoped. The team seemed sluggish, people were leaving at an alarming rate, and his department lagged behind others in the performance metrics used to determine management bonuses.

> "The first thing you need to hear is this: unless your people are desperate for the paycheck, they don't perform for you; they perform for themselves."

Bob was pretty frustrated with his team. He'd grown up in a military family, where people were simply expected to step up and get the job done. He'd hoped when he got into management that people would have the same respect for authority he'd shown his father. And in his management role, he'd always felt hampered by the "politically correct" HR directives. The style of management they preached seemed, well ... "namby pamby." He felt he was being asked to coddle his people rather than demand respect and obedience.

Bob loved his company's product. He was captivated by its technology and capabilities. He'd been promoted largely due to a great track record of individual commitment and performance. Now, after dealing with another week of "people issues," he found himself talking to his wife about taking a pay cut to get back down to the level where all he had to worry about was himself.

Bob had always regarded Dennis with a mixture of respect and envy. Dennis' department's responsibilities, size, and tasks were similar to Bob's. But Dennis' employees produced more and seemed happier than Bob's. They were, in Bob's estimation, clearly the kind who came to work with the right attitude and did as they were told. Bob was convinced HR was just hiring better people to work with Dennis. He complained both to his V.P. and to HR about the inequity. The answer came back that the same process is used to select all employees.

Due to shifting workloads, one of Bob's employees, Martin, was reassigned to Dennis' department. Bob took silent pleasure in the reassignment, for Martin was one of his "problem children." Over dinner with his wife, Bob said, "Now Dennis will know what it's like to work with the kinds of losers I've had to manage. We'll see what his bonus check looks like now that the playing field has been leveled."

Several months later, Bob stopped by Dennis' office. Smiling, he asked, "So, how's Martin working out?" Bob relished the opportunity to hear Dennis complain about an unproductive employee.

But Dennis said, "He's doing great! Thanks for letting me have him!"

Stunned, Bob said weakly, "You're welcome." He thought to himself, "I guess people can change. It would have been nice if Martin had gotten his act together before leaving my department."

But Bob's self-serving thought process began to break down as he faced an uncomfortable possibility: perhaps he was the problem. He swallowed his pride and asked Dennis to lunch.

Bob took Dennis to the sandwich shop across the street and found a quiet corner to talk. He came right to the point.

"Dennis, I'm really frustrated about finding good employees. I go home wondering why people don't seem to care as much as I do about the company. I feel like I'm always pushing people to get them to do their jobs right. I see your department and I don't know what you're doing differently. I've been thinking about going back to a non-supervisory role, but before I do, I just want to make sure I'm not missing something. So my question is this: how do you get people to perform for you?"

Dennis leaned back in his chair. After a moment, he looked Bob in the eye and said, "Well, the first thing you need to hear is this: unless your people are desperate for the paycheck, they don't perform for you; they perform for themselves. You are trying to get people to do things your way, and to live up to your standards. The problem is you think your people will only do what they're told. In fact, they want to do much more than that."

Bob was silent for a few minutes as he took it all in. "*I hope you don't have to get back to work right away, Dennis,*" *he said.* "*This could be a long conversation.*"

Find Buried Teasure

To motivate is to create motion, action, and results

The root of the word motivate is the same as the root word for "motive." What is a motive? It's a reason, a cause, a purpose for action. If I'm motivated to do something, it means I have a reason to do it.

Of course, some of your employees' motives at work might be pretty basic. Maybe they're afraid of starving – they live so close to the edge that losing their job would put them on the streets. Maybe they're so insecure that they put up with being bored or manipulated just to get tossed the occasional bone of thanks or support.

Maybe they're just frozen where they are – change is just too tough for them. So is risk. So they show up on time and do as they're told.

Is this the kind of employee you hunger for? If all you want is compliance, obedience, and dependability, you'll like these folks! But a manager who's looking to compete, to grow, to achieve a vision – a manager who wants his team to pursue complex challenges with initiative and creativity – might find the employees described above far less than suitable.

The fact is the world is changing. Especially in developed countries, the fundamental contract between employee and employer has evolved as these societies have become more affluent. Because the basic needs of most people are met, and because most qualified employees have many choices of where to work, the role of leaders in motivating people has become both more challenging and more exciting. No longer are most people willing to work just for the paycheck. No longer are people satisfied with simply doing as they're told. People want more. The enlightened leader understands how to effectively motivate people who want growth, opportunity, and challenge in the workplace.

In addition, the competitive landscape now only rewards companies that bring out the best in their employees. We call this "Finding Buried Treasure." In this plank, we'll explore the nature of motivation and the role of leadership in creating conditions that motivate.

Over the past 40 years or so, businesses have become more enlightened about the need to treat employees with respect and humanity. Workplace laws and common practice have eliminated most of the obviously abusive and dehumanizing aspects of the workplace. Managers are encouraged to "treat employees well" and to "bring out the best" in them.

But despite these shifts in thinking, an alarming number of people are fundamentally dissatisfied with their bosses. (Surveys put this number typically at 50-60%.) It's said that people don't leave jobs; they leave bosses. So, while we've tried to change the fundamental contract, most employees aren't happy with the results – and turnover rates reflect it.

Where are we falling short?

Despite creating better working conditions, many employers still primarily target pay, benefits, and incentive compensation as the best way to attract and retain productive employees.

So first, let's say a few words about those strategies:

- Of course, you need a competitive pay structure to attract quality. You need to compensate people at a level that allows them a fighting chance to create economic security for themselves.

- Having said that, pay ranks farther down on the list of desired attributes for employees than most managers realize. Raising pay and other benefits is a deficient and expensive way to "make up" for working conditions that an employee finds unattractive – and foremost among these unattractive conditions is a lousy boss.

- In fact, the data suggest people are actually de-motivated by incentive programs. The reasons:

    - Employees see them as controlling – an effort to get them to do something they wouldn't otherwise be disposed to do.

- Some incentive programs – especially involving internal competition – reward individualistic behavior. This discourages teamwork, which study after study finds to be a prerequisite for quality. It also can encourage employees to sweep bad news under the rug.

- Incentives can send the message that a particular task or project is not worth doing for its own sake. If it were, why would I need the bribe? Thus, in the employee's mind, incentives can actually devalue the work that the incentive is attempting to value.

So I encourage you to create an interesting and competitive pay package for your employees. But I suggest you consider this:

Financial compensation should be seen as an exchange of economic value between employee and employer. It's the "share" the employee receives for their work, and should not be considered a primary motivator.

Go ahead and disagree. It's true that many people choose jobs – or stay in jobs – because the pay is very good. But this is very different from saying the pay provides motivation to do one's best work. The research indicates people have other reasons to do well, and most of those reasons are intrinsic. If money is your primary tool for motivation, you might well be paying more than you need to for the performance you desire.

Managers who can create a motivating environment without relying primarily on pay are the managers who create the most value for their employees, their customers, and their companies.

What do you believe about the fundamental nature of people?

A debate has always raged over whether people are inherently lazy. Which side of this argument you come down on probably says a lot about your leadership approach.

If you, like Bob above, believe that most people will avoid work or responsibility if they can, then you'll probably embrace a style of leadership that relies on control and dominance to police these inherently lazy people. You'll likely look to blame someone when things go wrong, assuming that most problems are caused by people who don't share your work ethic. You are probably guarded, suspicious, and pessimistic.

If, on the other hand, you believe people on the whole are inclined to be responsible, hard-working, and self-motivated, then your style of leadership will likely be more collaborative, open, and trusting. This doesn't imply you'll be a pushover – just that you'd rather assume the best than assume the worst. Because of this, you tend to grant your employees greater autonomy, self-determination, and responsibility. You know that sometimes people will let you down, but you also know most people are more productive in an environment that values them, trusts them, and encourages them to achieve something meaningful. So in the long term, you'll be more often pleased than disappointed.

Stop here for a minute and consider which type of person you are. I strongly suggest that the best leaders come to work seeing their employees as a potential source of treasure, and they relish the opportunity to find that treasure. These leaders also experience the sense of gratification and joy that comes from seeing their people reach their full potential – a potential that can't be realized by people who feel controlled and manipulated. Great leaders have a way of taking employees other managers have dismissed and getting great results from them.

It's not a black or white thing

Of course, the debate over whether people are fundamentally lazy is, in the end, a debate centering on two extremes of human behavior. No one is completely lazy or completely productive. The best approach is realistic optimism.

Extrinsic and Intrinsic Motivation

These are two of the most important terms to understand as you learn to create an environment of positive motivation.

"Extrinsic" refers to factors outside of ourselves that we allow to affect our behavior. Extrinsically focused people are not self-determining. They believe that their outcomes in life are a result of things over which they have no control. As a result they don't hold themselves accountable for their performance.

We are *all* extrinsically focused to some degree. How many of us sometimes blame a gray day for a bad mood, or an unkind comment from someone as an excuse for our own boorish behavior?

How many of us, when things go wrong, look hard to find some extrinsic excuse?

- I don't get paid enough to do this job well.
- I don't do my best work on Mondays.
- I was distracted by others and so I forgot to return your phone call.
- My boss doesn't want me to succeed.

Part of developing leadership is recognizing when you – or others – are avoiding accountability by leaning on extrinsic factors.

But aren't extrinsic factors sometimes the cause of failures? Well of course, yes, but it's the pattern of thinking we're talking about here. If your inclination is to look first to extrinsic factors to explain your situation or performance, then you're not living up to your responsibility as a leader. The first inclination of the leader is to take an intrinsic view.

Intrinsic thinking calls us to explore our own impact on what has happened, and to use our own resources to find satisfaction and to move forward in a positive way. We ask one fundamental question over and over: *What am I going to do about it?*

As an intrinsic thinker, you don't give your power away to external events and the actions of others. You have your own reasons for living your life in a certain way, and they are reason enough. Because you are comfortable with your place in the world, you are grounded enough to open to others' perspectives and thus to find common ground. As an intrinsic thinker, you are self-aware, self-directed, and accountable in the truest sense of the word.

Intrinsic thinkers are motivated from the feelings they generate from doing well. The intrinsic thinker embraces work as fun and fulfilling, and regards difficulties as learning opportunities – welcomed challenges to their abilities or their character.

Intrinsic satisfaction can also result from taking action because our values direct us to do so – for example, bestowing charity or protection on those less fortunate. If you scratch the surface of a generous person, you may find a person who finds satisfaction in living their values.

Whether motivated by enjoyment or by a sense of healthy obligation, an intrinsic thinker receives a positive emotional payoff from a job well done. Others can reinforce these feelings for you, but they are sourced in your own intentions and your own integrity.

Above all, leaders take responsibility. Extrinsic thinkers cannot lead effectively because in their minds, the locus of responsibility exists outside of them. The effective leader continually develops an intrinsic focus.

To a large degree, a leader is a person who believes their reality is largely of their own making. They believe in a kind of karmic contract with the world – that doing the right thing and taking responsibility will eventually reward them with success. Leaders who observe themselves or others engaging in extrinsic thinking should challenge it whenever appropriate.

Again, the leader is a positive realist. Sometimes extrinsic factors are difficult to anticipate. Kids get sick, trucks break down, computers crash, and other people drop the ball. But to a degree even these types of events can be anticipated and managed. When events occur, the extrinsic thinker looks for the excuse; the intrinsic thinker looks for solutions, lessons learned, and growth from the experience.

The emotional intrinsic payoff is much more powerful for employees – over the long run – than the extrinsic payoff. So leaders always do what they can to foster intrinsic satisfaction first and foremost. This is fundamental to your understanding of motivation. Employees in our society have largely advanced beyond the need for basic security. More people than ever before are asking to be intellectually fed and challenged in the workplace. They are asking because it's an emotionally satisfying process to do work that has meaning and interest for them – work that allows them to prove their worth and exhibit their full range of talents. They are no longer willing to see themselves as cogs in a machine.

This is what we must respond to in our leadership. And statistics indicate most managers haven't mastered it yet. Too many people are feeling disconnected, uncertain of the meaning of their career, and unable to connect with their highest sense of purpose and values.

They long for managers who will help them do exactly that.

Our employees and colleagues therefore present us with both a great challenge and a great opportunity. The challenge is to develop the skills to motivate an increasingly sophisticated workforce that doesn't simply "go along." The opportunity is to find the buried treasure of our workforce – to see how lives can change and organizations can transform when people find intrinsic meaning in their work.

The 6 Shovels of Motivation

- **Fit**
- **Meaning**
- **Connection**
- **Growth**
- **Self-Determination**
- **Context**

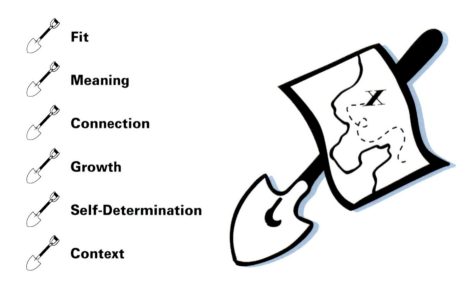

The 6 "Shovels" To Unearth the Treasure

1. Fit

Your intellect, disposition, and attitude predispose you to be good at certain things and not so good at others; interested in certain things, less interested in others. It takes work to find the right match between you and your work – but it's just as important for a person to find the right work "fit" as it is to find a good life partner.

The art and science of hiring well sets the stage for a motivating environment. People are naturally motivated to do well when their work fits their personality and their interests.

I know, for example, that I have the intellectual capacity and the aptitude with numbers to be an accountant. But I wouldn't be a good accountant, at least not for very long, because the work simply doesn't fit my personality. I find it difficult to stay focused on a project for an entire day, and I work best when I'm performing a variety of tasks. I also tend to skip important details in pursuit of the "big picture." I would probably be a sloppy and ineffective accountant.

The qualities that would make me a bad accountant have little to do with my intellect, my attitude, my work ethic, or my ability to communicate, so it's conceivable I could interview well for an accountant position. If the employer weren't aware of the "fit" issue, they might end up with me – an accountant who would struggle to motivate myself and who would probably leave for the first available job that fit me better.

How do you evaluate "fit"? Many interview techniques can help, and I suggest you become a student of interview techniques in any case. Finding out what a person does in his spare time can be an important clue, as can asking about long-term career goals.

There is also a number of very effective personality–based assessments. Some of these assessments use a "benchmarking" system that provides a strong indication of fit.

Our tendency when staffing our team is to look for talent, experience, personality, energy, and a good job reference. A person can have all of these things in spades and still be a bad fit to the particular job. And no matter how good a motivator you think you are, you won't get long-term quality from someone who doesn't fit her job responsibilities.

This is the most intrinsic of motivators – the desire to do work aligned with our interests and our style. Good leaders work hard to create this fit between person and profession.

2. Meaning

Whether we realize it or not, we all long to be part of something bigger than ourselves. This provides us a sense of meaning for work that might otherwise appear pointless.

One of my clients makes parts for airplanes. If you saw these parts sitting on workbenches in their factory, you'd have no idea what they were for. They come through the plant with a number identifier or a cryptic description. Employees could easily see these parts as "widgets" unconnected to any meaningful purpose.

But these items eventually are integrated into multi-million-dollar commercial airplanes. The company has many pictures of these airplanes under construction, showing where their parts are installed. They also occasionally take employees on plant tours to witness the installation. In the end, even the entry-level employee at this company can look with pride at a commercial airplane and say, "I helped build that plane."

Employees also derive satisfaction and meaning from helping others – from leading, mentoring, or teaching.

Work is meaningful when it is something more than a commercial endeavor. Even though no company can survive without making money, much of what motivates employees is a sense of pride – a sense that they have contributed something that generates more than just a paycheck.

Ask yourself how well you are helping to create meaning for your employees. Even the person who sweeps the floor or cleans the bathroom should take pride and derive meaning from their work. What do clean floors mean in your business? Does a clean floor create a positive impression that helps with sales? Does a clean building improve productivity? Does it enhance safety? Does it help to attract employees or customers? Help your employees find more meaning than simply sweeping floors or bending metal into indecipherable shapes.

Employees who find meaning in their work will naturally find intrinsic reasons to do well.

3. Connection

Creating meaningful personal connections is also a primary intrinsic motivator for most people. As we discussed in Plank 2, the human animal is intensely social – we strongly desire relationships of trust and familiarity with others.

Friendship in the workplace is different from other types of friendship (more on that later), but it is friendship indeed.

And that friendship extends to each employee's relationship with you, their leader. If their connection with you is warm and sincere, they will be motivated to please you and help you achieve your goals. There is an emotional payoff to helping a friend. Putting one's work in the context of helping friends creates accountability and a sense of positive obligation.

Many leaders fail to make these connections, especially with people who have unfamiliar cultural backgrounds, life circumstances, or interests. Often leaders fall too readily into work relationships that are easy and familiar, and miss out on the treasure to be found in connecting with "challenging people."

I live and work in an area that has a high percentage of immigrant workers. At my local shopping mall, I can hear four or more different languages spoken in a single day. And while it may be more difficult for me to make connections with these people than with a guy who loves baseball and grew up in suburbia, these connections are well worth making.

I once had an employee who loved drag racing. I would rather have major dental surgery than attend a drag race. But I often asked my employee about drag racing; I showed interest in the sport. Was this manipulative or dishonest? No – because I was interested not in the drag races but in the employee. By learning about drag racing I was learning about him. Through drag racing we forged a connection. We ended up having a warm and open relationship.

I get intrinsically motivated when I have the opportunity to work with people I like and admire, and who get me. Leaders who work hard to make these connections find it easier to build trust – and easier to give and receive feedback as a result.

The work of "connecting" with employees may feel like a waste of time to business people. In the hectic pace in which we operate, it takes a strong intention and solid time management to give this activity its proper priority. It is as important a "sandal" activity as anything else you do.

A piece of advice – these connections are best made on your schedule. Put a little wandering time into your calendar each day. It will help employees feel connected to you and make it less likely that they will disrupt your schedule later in the day.

Connections can also be fostered between the employee and the community in which they work. Businesses are a powerful engine for positive change in the world and for responsible activism on such issues as poverty, education, and the environment. Companies that encourage participation in activities that benefit the community – or the world – are helping employees to become better people, and to experience the deeper meaning of work.

4. Growth

People don't get up in the morning seeking to be incompetent. Most people prefer to be good at what they do, and to be proud of their work.

The quest for competence is a powerful motivator.

Leaders foster the personal and professional growth of those around them. They know that when employees are experiencing personal growth and developing mastery, their confidence is being enhanced by their work, and they will want to come back for more.

I can think of several people who have really stretched and challenged me in my career. It wasn't always pleasant; sometimes it was downright scary. But I knew that something important was happening, and I felt honored and trusted by these leaders who exhibited confidence in me.

Growth is a difficult thing to modulate with employees. It's easy to overextend people with tasks or projects beyond their current capacity. A good rule of thumb is "110%." Ask your employees to work 10% beyond their current capacity – and then coach and monitor the effort. This provides them the motivation of seeing their skills and capabilities increase – without setting them up for failure.

Some people are so afraid of risk that they don't want to learn anything new. They're afraid they'll fail in the new task or project. Growth should not be optional; even the most risk-averse employee must be challenged to grow. An organization whose employees are stagnant will not survive.

Formal training has many benefits – not the least of which is the motivational value of growing on the job. Immediately applying a newly acquired skill is a powerful way to retain the learning; it's also a powerful motivational tool.

Effective leaders see their employees (and themselves) as works in progress. Remember the child who ties his shoes for the first time, smiles, and shouts, "Look what I can do!" We never lose that sense of delight, though it gets dampened by adult responsibilities. Bring it back to your workplace and you'll see motivation rise.

As part of an employee's overall growth, cross-training is one of the great win-wins in business. It encourages the development of new skills, it helps people understand and respect one another's work, it fosters teamwork, it encourages the improvement of processes, and it protects against business disruptions due to absences.

All of your employees should be learning something new all the time.

5. Self-determination

While no business is a true democracy, elements of democracy can and should be brought into the business environment.

Employees who have no voice in the direction of the department or the company become frustrated and unmotivated. One of our most powerful drives is to be self-determining – to have some semblance of power and control over our environment. Giving employees a say is essential.

A word of caution: giving the appearance of democracy without actually living it can destroy trust. It's important to tell employees when a decision will truly be determined by a vote, or when instead management is seeking input for a decision that will eventually be made at a higher level. Most of all, whenever seeking input, it's critical to really listen to what comes back.

Even when management ends up making the decision, employees' self-determination will be enhanced if they feel their ideas and concerns have been heard – and if employee influence was seen in the outcome. Employees aren't necessarily looking to have it their way. They just want to know that they have a say, and that someone above is listening.

LEAN Manufacturing and other continuous improvement processes have taught for years that employees should be heavily involved in determining the best work flows and business processes. A staff in which everyone thinks is a dynamic staff. As we've discussed, thinking can be hard work; but thinking aimed at improving one's circumstances is an act of self-determination. People who do so will be more motivated to perform and to grow.

6. Context

People very much want to know what's going on – in the department, in the company, and even in the larger marketplace in which the company competes.

Leaders need to understand that this is an issue of trust. If employees don't know the truth about what's going on, they'll make up their own truths. It's better for them to have the facts – even unpleasant ones – than to make up their own.

Years ago, I was asked to turn around a failing business. In the 12 months prior to my arrival, the company had lost $600,000. The first thing I did was call an all-employee meeting. At the top of the agenda was this question: "How many of you think this business is profitable?"

Of 35 employees, 32 raised their hands. I wondered how management had expected to solve a problem that only a few people even knew existed. I also knew that motivation was a big problem in this organization.

Managers often assume that sharing bad news will demoralize employees. And certainly, news of a major layoff, or the loss of the company's largest customer, or of a major restructuring that might require relocation, is difficult to deal with. But employees are not children, and they resent being treated as such. When you withhold information – even of a disturbing nature – employees feel distrusted and marginalized.

The 32 employees in the story above were disturbed to find out their business was losing money. They were even embarrassed to have been ignorant of such important data. But I invited them to be a part of the solution. Within hours they were coming to me with ideas to make things better. Dealing with this difficulty in an open and collaborative way made us a stronger team.

In the rush of work, sometimes leaders simply forget to keep their employees in the loop. But regardless of the news – a new set of lunchroom furniture, a change in coffee suppliers, a new shipment of computers, or a visit from the top brass – employees want to know what's going on.

Employees who know what's going on will often have something to contribute. And managers who are out in front of the news can communicate it in the way they see fit.

Businesses are Petri dishes for rumors. Management needs to understand its role in creating the rumor mill by deliberately withholding information that impacts employees.

Of course there are confidential issues that can't be shared – issues of a personal nature, or information that might disrupt a negotiation or a deal. But businesses that fail to communicate effectively with employees will find that their employees perform poorly. In addition to feeling marginalized and distrusted, they won't have the opportunity to be part of the solution.

Informed employees are generally motivated employees.

A word about morale and motivation

I have been struck by the fact that many companies have high morale and relatively low motivation.

It's important to attend to the morale of the troops – their pride in the company's products and their sense of belonging to something worthwhile. Morale is necessary for motivation. But it is not sufficient for motivation. Remember that motivation is forward motion. An organization with high morale may be resting on its laurels – may be overly conservative and resistant to change.

A company that has walls full of plaques and that constantly engages in happy talk about itself may be a company living in the past. Make sure your organization is motivated to change and grow.

One of the great gifts of leadership is the opportunity to see others do well. Motivated employees will take their satisfaction home and spread it in their families and communities. A true leader gets intrinsic satisfaction in helping others develop intrinsic satisfaction – and thus to do extraordinary things. As leadership theorist Peter Senge says, "The truly committed can accomplish the seemingly impossible."

The gifts and talents of those around us are buried treasures of the richest kind. Learn to unearth these treasures. Then stand back and watch the wonderful things they bring to you and your organization. Recognize that the hard work of creating fit, meaning, connection, growth, self-determination, and context for others will boost productivity far more than handing out bonus checks. With a highly motivated workforce, bonus checks will be the trailing indicator of success – not the cause of it.

Making It Real
Understand What Motivates Your Team

Make a list of the five direct reports or peer group team members with whom you work most closely.

For each of these people answer the following:

Referring to the six motivating behaviors outlined in Plank 5, what changes will I make in my interactions with this person to create a more motivational working environment for both of us?

Briefly describe the actions you will take with each individual, your reasoning for the actions, and the expected outcomes.

Schedule these actions into your calendar. How will you assess your – and their – progress?

Plank 6

Build Influence

I seek to teach and influence rather than control

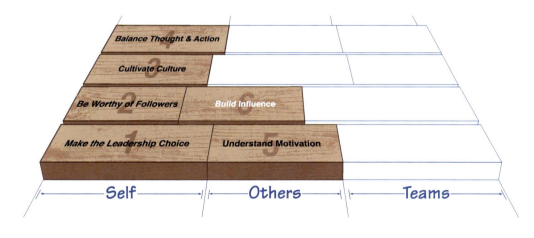

Bob and Sarah disagreed on whether Dorman Manufacturing should expand its warehouse, and with it, its inventory of finished goods. They both had strong opinions – and facts to back them up.

Bob and Sarah had comparable levels of authority in the company. They both reported to Ryan, who would ultimately make the decision on the warehouse expansion.

Bob felt the costs of the expansion would not justify the return. He was well-studied in supply chain management and the industry trend to limit finished goods in favor of a "real-time" management system. He had done considerable analysis, using historical and projected sales figures, and concluded the new warehouse space would not meet a compelling financial need.

Bob was sure he had all the facts he needed to shoot down the warehouse expansion in the name of a safe and sane approach to growth. He respected Sarah, but he was looking forward to watching Ryan choose his direction rather than Sarah's. Bob saw this as a competition, albeit a friendly one.

In the weeks leading to the decision, Bob stayed mainly in his office, preparing his case and polishing his presentation. During this time, he saw Sarah operating in her usual outgoing, collaborative way. He noted she made a number of trips into Ryan's office. But Bob wasn't worried – his case was open and shut.

Influence is the art of working with people to develop the understanding and support needed to enact change.

Sarah told Bob she supported the warehouse expansion as a leap of faith that would invigorate sales growth. She acknowledged the risks, but she downplayed them. The larger inventory, Sarah felt, would put Dorman in a favored position because of the company's increased capacity to provide just-in-time deliveries. She also pointed out that Dorman's margins were likely to go up thanks to higher levels of service, and that the carrying costs of inventory were not as high as a few years ago, thanks to low interest rates.

Bob and Sarah both had good business minds. They both had good frameworks for evaluating the warehouse expansion decision. When given the opportunity to present his analysis, Bob delivered a compelling presentation to Ryan and the leadership team. He felt confident he'd "won."

Thus Bob was devastated and angry when Ryan decided to move forward with the expansion.

The day after the decision, Bob was moping over a cup of coffee when Sarah walked in. Bob looked up. "Congratulations," he said, mustering every ounce of graciousness he could. "Looks like you're the big winner." After a breath, he added, "How did you manage to convince Ryan?"

Sarah sat down and looked him in the eye. "First of all," she said, "I don't see it as a personal win for me and a loss for you, and you shouldn't either. You'll have a big part in the expansion project, and I know Ryan's looking to you to provide great project support."

"You know, Bob," she continued, "the Board is a little frustrated about slow growth. They're looking to take a few more risks. I talked to Ryan about his conservative approach, and suggested it might be time to hang his hat on a project like this. He was agonizing about the facts and the risks, but we finally agreed this was his chance to step up and make some bigger changes. I assured him I would stand by his decision and work to make it a win for him in the end."

Bob was furious. "'We' agreed? Who's 'we,' and why wasn't I involved in those discussions? I might not have made a fool of myself preparing a major presentation for something I was bound to lose on. And how fair is it that Ryan had these dialogs with you alone, and you ended up knowing things about the Board's position that I didn't know?"

Sarah countered, "Your facts were important – they made us more aware of the risks. But what should have been a risk analysis came across as you trying to convince Ryan you were smarter than anyone else. And you want to know how I knew things you didn't? It's because I get out and engage with people. I get myself on Ryan's calendar, and when I meet with him I ask a lot of questions to find out what's going on."

Bob looked down and said dismissively, "I just don't like to play those games. We should make decisions based on facts in this company. I like to think we don't play politics with important strategic matters."

Exasperated, Sarah got up to leave. On her way out, she stopped and turned toward Bob. "Look," she said, "what I did wasn't political, and it didn't contribute to a poor decision. Every decision is a product of both factual analysis and gut feelings. I was tuned in to the gut feelings and you weren't. I don't think that's manipulative or political on my part – I actually think it's good leadership."

Bob was confused. Not at all signed on to this decision, he secretly began hoping the warehouse expansion would fail. He felt he had done his job, thinking clearly about the options and presenting a great case for maintaining the warehouse in its current configuration – yet he'd ended up on the margins of this decision. Bob didn't understand how to expand his influence with Ryan beyond effectively presenting the critical facts. Ryan was a big boy, he thought, and shouldn't be so easily persuaded by Sarah and her "gut feelings."

What Bob didn't realize was that all three players in this drama – he, Sarah, and Ryan – had missed opportunities to create positive influence, teamwork, and buy-in on the decision. Ryan had opened his door to Sarah's influence but hadn't sought Bob out during the process. Sarah had wielded her influence with Ryan, but she'd lost an opportunity to get Bob's support and ownership on her idea, now that it was moving forward. And Bob, sitting in his office, had been oblivious to the influence Sarah was developing with their boss, and thus in the company. Had he been more interested in a positive outcome than a personal win, Bob might have recognized the value of all parties building influence with each other.

And now Ryan was going to need his help on a project on which Bob felt like an outsider. Had Ryan worked to maintain influential positions with Bob throughout the process, he might now count on that support. Instead, Ryan would probably be faced with having to direct Bob to support a project for which Bob was unlikely to accept accountability.

Earth & Moon

The measure of your leadership effectiveness will be your ability to drive positive change. To do so, you must have *influence* – the art of developing the understanding and support needed to enact change.

Teasing the word apart gives us clues to its meaning: in-fluence. What does it mean to be fluent in a language? It means you understand it and can exchange ideas and meanings with others through that language. Add the prefix "in-," and you can think of "influence" as helping others to "take understanding and meaning in" – or, to use more popular business terms, to take "ownership" or "buy in."

When we exert influence, we create understanding and meaning that then become part of another's intrinsic reasons for taking action.

The dictionary definition refers to the invisibility of influence – the person being influenced doesn't always know the source of the power that sways them to action. When influence results in people feeling stirred or called to act *from within themselves,* they are more motivated than when they perceive the call to action coming from the outside.

Thus it is always preferable, though not always possible, to incite action through this art of influence rather than though command and control. We've discussed (see Plank 5) the importance of intrinsic motivation, of action that is internally sourced as opposed to extrinsically cajoled or mandated. We know that people do best when they internalize and personalize the reasons for the work. Influence fosters this internalization and thus creates, over the long term, positive, sustainable results.

It's said that people don't resist change; people resist being changed. Unless the current state of affairs is distinctly and unacceptably painful, people are likely to avoid the uncertainty or fear that imposed change creates. Here's why:

- Most people aren't visionary, so they fail to self-generate excitement and enthusiasm for something different.

- When change occurs, people's comfort and safety are threatened. Even if the old system doesn't work particularly well, people often feel it's "home."

- The call for change is often perceived as a condemnation of the old, or a labeling of past efforts as failures. It's difficult for some to change because they don't want to think they've been doing it "wrong" all these years.

- Change puts people on the growing edge, with all its discomfort and uncertainty. "Will I be able to learn what I need to learn? What if I'm not up to snuff? I'm so good at what I do now – do I really have to do it differently?"

- Often the old system has created great benefits in compensation, authority, and influence for some members of the organization. In the wake of change, those who've been doing well in the old system may lose income, privilege, authority, or stature.

All this means that to implement change, the leader must use all her skills – influence chief among them. Influence involves the hard work of developing ideas, refining them, selling them, and then selling them again. Influence depends on developing relationships of trust and then showing up authentically, passionately, and competently within those networks. Influence is about staying focused on what's important, capitalizing on what is shared, and then creating new meanings and new contexts.

What influence isn't:

- *Winning* at the expense of others – unless it is absolutely necessary. Playing hard ball is almost always a bad idea; it usually creates a short-term win and a long-term loss. (However, influence can be seen as winning if it's a *collective* win.)

- Manipulation or politics. In fact, I see positive influence as the opposite of politics. Politics in the workplace is self-serving behavior that is the natural outcome of a lack of shared vision. There is a "karma" factor here. By manipulating relationships and playing politics, you might again reap a short-term gain; but is it worth sowing bad energy and distrust?

- Being too patient. Building influence usually takes time, but in critical situations, you might have to wield a style of influence that conveys a sense of urgency. Just be aware that a heavy-handed, impatient approach will create damage that will need to be healed later.

It's not enough to be "right"

Do you ever feel you're "right" on an issue but can't persuade others to embrace your point of view? It's a common frustration, especially among younger leaders. And it reminds me of the surgeon who says, "The operation was a success, but the patient died."

As Bob found out in our story above, it doesn't always help to have better information or more insightful analyses. Being right isn't worth a whole lot if you can't bring others on board.

Maybe you've seen something go wrong in your organization, and you've found yourself saying (publicly or privately), "If only they'd listened to me – I could have told them ...." Or maybe, in a passive-aggressive way, you've allowed something to go south so you could prove others wrong.

If you see a train wreck coming, you have an obligation to try to prevent it. This isn't always possible, of course; someone else may have their hands so firmly on the controls that you can't slow the train or change its course. But if the accident occurred because you weren't able to influence others to see it coming, then you are complicit through a failure of leadership.

It's fun to be out in front of others, to discern when change is needed, to generate useful analyses and conclusions based on your ability to see things differently. The leader tries, through dialog that enhances collective intelligence, to produce as many right answers as possible. But right answers mean little unless the organization is called to action around them. That's where influence comes in.

If you find yourself on the sidelines, simply judging the rightness or wrongness of others' actions, then maybe it's time to get in the game.

The Moon and the Earth

The moon is tiny compared with Earth, and hundreds of thousands of miles away. Yet its essential influence on life on this planet is undeniable. Without the tides, life here might never have developed the way it did. Consider the analogy with influence in the business world:

1. The moon is powerful, but its power is felt indirectly.

In fact, it is only recently that science has come to understand the profound effect of the moon on the tides.

Power, which scholar Kenneth Boulding defines as "the ability to change the future," is a hot topic in the workplace, and in many ways the central concept in this plank. Is it good to be powerful? Of course it is, if your power meets two important criteria:

- You believe the benefit to others from the exercise of your power outweighs the harm.

- Your power most often takes the form of "power to…" and "power with…" rather than "power over."

Personal power is a hallmark of a good leader. Employees commonly complain their bosses aren't powerful enough. Assuming a leader is "worthy of followers," those followers very much want their bosses not to sit on the sidelines and not to be victims, but to "make things happen." This is how effective leaders are measured. Primarily through influence, they're able to generate momentum and action, even where others have failed.

Thus, to be powerful with positive intentions is the essence of leadership. But, like the moon, our leadership influence is not a direct application of force – or "power over" – but rather one that is felt indirectly.

2. Astronauts who have seen the Earth from the moon have an entirely new perspective on our planet – a view from an objective distance.

How much sooner would we have known the earth was round if we'd been able to see it from the moon! As we discussed in "Cultivate Culture" (Plank 3), leaders must be objective observers of their environment. This is only possible from a healthy distance.

How does this affect our ability to influence others? As objective observers, we avoid the territoriality, defensiveness, and blind spots that occur when we can't separate ourselves from our environment. So think of yourself as the moon, creating power and influence over the "planet" you work on while maintaining a healthy psychic distance from it.

3. The moon's small size in relation to the Earth doesn't stop it from exerting a powerful influence on the larger body.

We often fail to exert influence because we feel we're too "small." It's easy to feel intimidated by a real difference in rank, by a person with more vocal or aggressive style, or simply by our lack of self-confidence.

I spent 10 years in an organization of over 10,000 employees. Reflecting on that experience, I am proudest of the fact that I embraced opportunities to drive change even when the size of the organization (or the problem!) felt daunting. Naturally there were times when the large object just couldn't be moved. But I came away consistently surprised by the impact one person with a vision, confidence, and a patient and persistent approach could have. Buoyed by my experience, I now strongly encourage leaders to take the reins of change in service of their vision no matter how "small" they perceive themselves. And once again, building influence is the key.

Opening yourself to your own potential for influence is one thing; it's also important to open yourself to *being* influenced. In the eyes of your direct reports, you are the large object. Do your employees feel they can influence you? Do they even try? What environment have you created?

4. The moon's influence on the earth has a light touch. The moon, with all of its power and influence, doesn't create fear and intimidation.

No matter how clear, obvious, or persuasive your point of view, people respond poorly to coercion.

Influence is best experienced as choice by those who are being influenced. Again, this is not always possible. But the degree to which your influence taps into the intrinsic motivations of others will determine the quality and breadth of your influence.

This brings up a simple but profound characteristic of effective leaders: they put themselves in the shoes of those they aspire to lead. Leaders ask, "Why would anyone follow me, on this issue or in general?" Motivation, commitment, and influence all flow in large part from a leader's understanding of his audience. The ability to communicate and empathize with your team is essential to all aspects of leadership, but it's absolutely vital to the leader who wishes to enlarge his sphere of influence.

Stephen Covey and the Circles of Influence and Concern

Stephen Covey writes some of the best leadership literature we've seen. One simple yet compelling example of Covey's powerful ideas is the circle of influence and concern.

Covey draws a large circle to enclose everything we are actively concerned about – in life, work, family, the world. It's haunting to wonder how different the world might be if more people of principle placed more of the world's challenges inside their "circle of concern," and considered what role they might play in addressing them.

But it's not enough just to have care or concern about more of the issues around you. Within that larger circle of concern is a smaller concentric circle of what we can actually have influence over. When we expend mental energy on concerns that are outside our "circle of influence," we're worrying about things we can't do anything about. We're wasting our time.

But when we pull our concerns inside our circle of influence, we give ourselves the opportunity to take action. And in doing so, we exercise the muscles to push that circle outward, thus building our power, our influence. And if you look hard, you might be surprised to discover how many of your concerns you can pull into your circle of influence – even just by writing a letter to Congress, or donating a few dollars, or asking a colleague a well-placed question.

Let's say you aren't happy with the performance of a co-worker – someone who doesn't report to you. You might choose to do nothing but stew on it or complain about it, thus letting it impinge on your own productivity. In other words, you might leave it in your circle of concern, *outside* your circle of influence.

Of course, we have to be sensible about what concerns we choose to act on. You can't solve all the problems in the workplace, let alone the world. But for anything you choose not to act on, the healthy approach is to avoid expending mental energy on it. Save the energy for things you do choose to exert some influence over. This is another hallmark of a leader.

In this plank we ask you to consider how much good you might do by two simple acts: bringing more of the issues around you into your circle of concern, and then making the choice to take action on the pieces you might be able to influence.

> **Making It Real**
> *Growing Your Influence*
>
> Draw your own circles of influence and concern. Then map current people, issues, projects, activities, tasks, etc., onto the circles based on where they are right now in your mind. Include items in your professional life *and* your personal life. Then in a second diagram, re-map each of these items onto the circles the way you think they *could* or should be, so that you spend more time and activity within your zone of influence.
>
> Finally, describe the specific action steps you intend to take in order to bring certain items closer to your circle of influence. Include timeframes and a structure for holding yourself accountable to these commitments.

Influence and Stress

There is a paradox about taking the role of influencer. Many of us believe that by stepping back, not getting involved, and avoiding the risks of leadership, we avoid stress.

In fact, nothing is more stressful than powerlessness. My greatest stress occurs when I know I could do something to make things better, but I don't do it. Even small steps make a big difference in turning concerns into influence.

What do we call a problem that won't go away? A "nagging" problem. The term is fitting: an inner voice nags you to do something about it. How much less stressful would our lives be if we could get rid of that awful nagging inside our heads by taking action? For example:

- What if we addressed emerging conflicts early on, before trust is damaged?

- What if we exhibited more self-discipline on matters of personal health or time management?

- What if we took the time to solve a problem rather than constantly working around it?

How do we create positive influence?

So how do you measure up on the behaviors and attitudes of influential leaders? As you reflect on the list below, ask yourself how you might become more influential by developing your skills in each area.

Use what you have already learned in this book

Much of what we learned in Planks 1-5 applies to your ability to become more influential. And it's not enough just to read the plank chapters. You must put them into practice every day:

Plank 1 - Make the Leadership Choice. If you have vision, and you're taking the mantle of leadership on yourself in service of that vision, you'll spread your influence to others who will want to accompany you on that journey.

Plank 2 - Be Worthy of Followers. Developing your character, acting in integrity, and being aware of your "ripple effect" will set the stage for greater influence.

Plank 3 - Cultivate Culture. Your ability to see the culture of your organization objectively, and to understand its strengths and weaknesses, will help you communicate and lead change.

Plank 4 - Balance Thought and Action. By becoming a thoughtful leader – one who spends time in reflective work – you will understand more of what the organization needs, and you'll plot a course for achieving it. You'll become more effective at planning and articulating change and managing change efforts.

Plank 5 - Understand Motivation. Your ability to motivate people of course goes hand-in-hand with your ability to influence them. The more you connect people to their work, the more they'll understand the need for change, and the more effective they'll be at finding a useful and positive role for themselves in whatever change takes place.

Develop a Point of View

In order to be influential, you need to develop points of view, opinions, or theories. Many who aspire to be leaders never engage in the intellectual work of studying their environment creatively and analytically.

There are dozens of universal issues facing every business today. Just a few would make a challenging list – and these don't even take into account the issues specific to your business:

The changing work force – how are you planning for likely shortages of skilled labor in the years ahead?

Ownership transition – what will happen when your business makes a generational or ownership transition?

Technology – how is the emergence of new technologies creating competitive problems and opportunities?

Globalization – how affected are you likely to be by continuing globalization of services and products? How might it present both opportunities and challenges?

Managing inventory – how can your business minimize the losses and risks associated with unproductive inventories?

Peak oil – experts agree we're near the end of the age of cheap energy, as fossil fuel resources dwindle and become more costly to extract. What impact will accelerating energy costs have on your business, and how will you compensate?

Leaders *never let other people do their thinking for them*. It's the leader's job to ponder these questions, so as to steer the organization toward a safe harbor in a challenging business environment. If someone asked you the questions above, or other key questions about the future of your business, would you have a point of view to share? Even if you are a mid-level manager and not the chief executive, you'll expand your influence by gathering information and developing points of view.

And once you've developed a point of view:

Test it. Further reading on the subject (a simple internet search will probably give you everything you need), engaging in dialog with others, and watching responsible journalism on television can help test the validity of your perspective, developing and modifying it in a grounded way.

Sell it. Once you've established a point of view, and you've grounded it by testing its validity, be courageous about selling it. It bothers me to hear people say, "It's just my opinion." Don't devalue your points of view that way. What you think, observe, assess, and surmise is important to your organization. Be willing to share it – and then be willing to:

Defend it, adapt it, shelve it, or chuck it. Mature leaders are open to being influenced and thus willing to change their minds. The mature leader knows when to defend a point of view to the death, when to adjust it to fit reality, when to abandon it in deference to an alternative one, and when to put it on the shelf for later. How wrong of us to admire someone for "staying the course" long after their point of view has been discredited.

Have positive intentions

In any interaction with another person, it's a good gut check to ask yourself about your intentions. Bringing healthy, service-oriented intentions to your work with others is a key to influential behavior. Good or bad, your intentions reveal themselves to others pretty quickly.

- Are you looking for a win for both parties, or just trying to advance your own agenda?

- Are you seeking to share your information and insight for the benefit of all, or are you trying to prove you're smarter?

- Are you trying to advance your career and compensation, or are you truly trying in some way to advance the "common good"? (Not to imply that these are always in opposition.)

Positive intentions create positive influence. If people trust your intentions, they are more likely to follow you across gaps and into the future.

Be patient and persistent

Great initiatives for change often fail because leaders lose focus or simply give up too quickly. Experience in leadership teaches us that things take time. It's critical to balance your desire to see change happen now with your ability to discern what the organization will tolerate.

This is part of the art of leadership: knowing when to push and when to pull back and try again later. You'll be guided by the criticality of the situation. If the organization is in crisis, patience isn't a virtue – persistence is.

Typically, messages of change are not fully comprehended in a single swipe. Good leaders know the value of repeating themselves. If you think you're pushing too hard, ask your team. In my experience, leaders often overestimate the quality and quantity of their effort in leading change, so they run out of steam, despairing that "no one gets it around here." If people aren't getting it, there's a good chance you're not giving it enough.

Change is difficult. Hold yourself accountable for making it happen, but understand that changing hearts and minds requires a long-term commitment and a willingness to go back to the well time and time again.

Be pragmatic

The world needs idealists. They form visions, and we've seen how important vision is to leadership. But idealists often flame out and crash in a world that also requires a pragmatic approach.

Pragmatism is defined as "concern with practical consequences or values." Being pragmatic means we take a step-by-step, real-world approach to getting things done, taking into account the capabilities and interests of all stakeholders as well as systemic influences that go far beyond our team or even our organization. And we don't expect other people to be blown away by our brilliance and kick into immediate, sustained action based solely on our vision of a better future.

Idealism and pragmatism are the ultimate combination. Idealism and *perfectionism,* on the other hand, are a lethal mix – you'll be perpetually discouraged by a world that simply fails to meet your grand visions and high expectations.

Your task as a leader: assess what can be done, plan the steps necessary to do it, and then diligently and patiently get into action.

Be passionate

The word passion comes from the Latin root "passio," meaning "suffering." The most inspiring leaders care enough to endure suffering in pursuit of their vision. When others see this in you, they will be influenced.

Imagine your boss has no emotion at all around a leadership initiative. Ask yourself if you would take risks, endure change, or work hard for that effort. Our leaders, through their actions, their focus, their tone, and their choice of priorities, signal the importance of the problems and opportunities they face. To be influenced, we need to believe they have some skin in the game – that what they're asking us to do is important to them.

But sometimes as leaders we are asked to lead a change effort for which we have little passion. When this happens, try to find something to attach your passion to.

Once I was asked to shut down a retail operation that had suffered for years under the curse of a dismal location. I shared with my team a distinct lack of enthusiasm for shutting down something we'd worked hard to build. But we gathered together and asked ourselves what was important in the process. We agreed on two things: we would try to retain as many customers as possible by encouraging them to shop at one of our other locations, and we would walk away with pride in having done a terrific job on an unsavory task. By resetting our objectives, we were able to experience positive emotions – even passion – in our work.

It's critically important to create a positive emotional climate around any work that needs to be done, especially when that work is particularly challenging. Showing passion for the work helps you influence others to do the same.

Present persuasively

To sell your point of view, it's not enough to discuss it casually in the lunchroom, or to bring it up as Item 15 on the agenda of a long meeting. Your investment in creating influence is reflected in your willingness to get your thoughts down on paper or in presentation form, so you can make the most cogent, persuasive, and – yes – passionate case for your ideas.

Fear of making our points of view public, or inability to create effective written, visual, or oral presentations, are common reasons people fail to gain influence. If you believe in your point of view, then presenting it to others is a great way to test it, to foster dialog that helps refine it, and to develop understanding and support for it.

Making It Real
Mapping Your Influence Potential

Draw an "influence map" showing all the people and issues you feel you need to positively influence in order to fulfill your leadership potential. Map out the specific behaviors that might help you gain that influence. Then add time frames to those behaviors you're willing to commit to in the next few weeks or months, and describe how you'll hold yourself accountable for making good on those commitments.

Influence is something good leaders cultivate because they know it's critical for achieving what they want to accomplish. Developing influence with others is your way of honoring and serving your vision. If you aren't influencing others, you either lack vision or you lack the will or skills to advance your vision. You can have a pretty good career without much influence, but if the leadership flame burns in you, you'll need to diligently maximize your ability to influence others.

Plank 7

Connect With Meaning

I seek authenticity and depth in my relationships

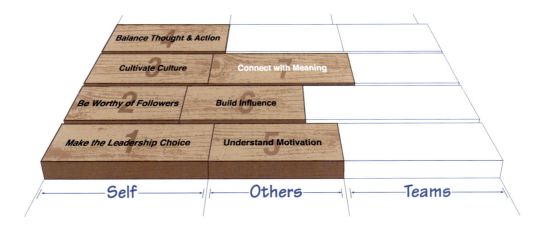

Tom had just finished his marketing presentation at the Leadership Team meeting. He'd been working hard on it for several weeks. He knew his ideas had strategic merit, and he had supported his case with facts and considerable analysis. Now he was hoping for constructive feedback, especially from Tony, his boss.

When Tom finished the presentation, Tony stood and moved to the front of the room. "Thanks, Tom," he said in less than an enthusiastic tone of voice. "Now let's move on to a discussion of last month's sales figures."

Tom was furious. He felt dismissed, even a bit humiliated. After the meeting, several colleagues came up and in a sympathetic tone said, "Thanks," or "Good job." But Tom had wanted Tony's acknowledgement and approval.

Tom waited several days, hoping Tony would follow up with him. But there was not an email, not a phone message – nothing from Tony. Tom's frustration and sense of betrayal increased daily.

Finally Tom walked into Tony's office and sat down. Tony looked up from his papers with a questioning glance and said, "Can we make this fast?"

"Okay," Tom said, "I'll make it fast. I put in a lot of work on the Leadership Team presentation and I haven't heard so much as a peep out of you. Did I screw up?"

Tony put down his papers. "Oh geez, didn't Paul talk to you yet?" Paul, the Director of Finance, held the purse strings for the budget Tom needed to move forward. "I thought the presentation was fantastic! I asked Paul to huddle up with you to develop a budget for your program."

What appears to be harmony may be passive acceptance of mediocrity.

Tom was silent for a moment. Then he said, "Tony, I've spent the last four days in a funk because I thought you didn't give a damn about my ideas. Am I really so bad at reading you?"

Tony laughed. "No, and I'm sorry. I was so focused on the next agenda item that I didn't acknowledge your presentation. I'm under some hellacious pressure right now to open up the Denver office, and I was truly distracted." He stood up and offered his hand. "I look forward to watching your program become a huge success. And next time you're in a funk, don't wait four days before you talk to me, okay?"

Tom smiled. He knew Tony should have done a better job of communicating, both at the meeting and in the days following. But he also realized it had been counterproductive on his part to assume the worst without reaching out to find the truth.

Gina had just adjourned her weekly management meeting and rushed back to her office to address pressing priorities. After a few minutes, Randy, her Office Manager, knocked on her door.

"Come on in, Randy," Gina said. "But I only have a minute."

"This will be fast," said Randy. "I just wanted to ask what's wrong. You usually do such a great job facilitating our meetings. You weren't at your best this morning. We missed our usual energetic and purposeful boss."

Gina hesitated. She thought about telling Randy about her short night's sleep and her long to-do list. She thought about mentioning the lengthy report she had to present to her boss later that day. But she didn't. Instead she looked at Randy and said, "Thanks for saying something about it. I did rush through things today and I didn't give you my best."

At one level, Gina had known her performance at the meeting had been poor, but until Randy challenged her on it, she didn't hold herself accountable for what the team had experienced. With Randy's comments, Gina suddenly understood that people really depended on her to bring her best to their meetings.

If Randy hadn't said anything, she might have allowed herself to continue to skate through future meetings. This brief conversation turned out to be one she remembered for the rest of her career. In the years that followed, she rarely brought anything less than her best to her management team meetings.

Sonja felt completely overwhelmed. And now, to top it off, Angela, her boss, was on the phone with a brand new project and an immediate deadline. As Angela explained what needed to be done, Sonja grabbed a red pencil and angrily crossed out all the top priorities on her to-do list. She was falling further and further behind. Sonja hated letting people down; her sense of loyalty and service to the company were legendary. However, she tended to suffer in silence, feeling isolated and unappreciated.

Angela asked if Sonja had any questions. Sonja paused, then said, "No – no questions." When they hung up, Sonja looked out the window for a minute, lost in thought. Then she picked up the phone and called Angela back.

"Angela," Sonja said, "I can't do it."

"Why not?" said Angela. "You need more information? Want me to send you a project plan?"

"I don't mean the project. I just can't do this anymore. I'm tired of being so far behind. I feel like I'm letting everyone down. I hate going home every day making excuses for why I didn't make as much progress as I should. You and everyone else are giving me more than I can handle – you don't understand the other things I'm also responsible for."

For a moment there was silence as Angela tried to digest what Sonja had said. Finally she said, "You know, Sonja, we're all busy."

Sonja's sense of duty came rushing back in. For a moment, she was tempted to apologize and offer to "suck it up" one more time. But she didn't. Instead she said, "Maybe that's the problem. We're running around trying to please one another, but we don't really talk about what's most important – or work on what's most important. There has to be a better way to manage our workloads."

Angela told Sonja she'd think about it some more. She was irritated, because she too was overworked and falling further and further behind. Sonja's comments cut a little bit close, perhaps.

Although the conversation did not provide a quick resolution, Sonja was relieved she had shared her feelings with Angela. When stress and confusion reigned in the organization, it needed to be aired. Sonja sent Angela a follow-up email with suggestions for improving their communication and for prioritizing their work together. She didn't know if anything would change, but even suggesting change felt better to her than staring out the window in despair.

Terry had applied for three promotions in the last year. Each time he had been passed up. Each time, his boss Ray had told him he was a good employee, and it was only a matter of time before Terry would get his opportunity.

Terry came from a family with high expectations. Promotions were important to him as a measure of his worth and a symbol to his family that he was successful. Trusting Ray's encouragement, he continued to do his work diligently, while patiently awaiting his promotion.

Finally, a suitable position opened up. Terry applied, thinking he had a real chance. And when Ray called him into his office and closed the door behind them, Terry thought this was the moment.

But Ray didn't offer him the promotion, and this time he didn't just give Terry bland encouragement. Instead, he screwed up the courage to tell Terry that he lacked some of the key skills and behaviors the company was looking for, and that his star was unlikely to rise any further. Ray said he hoped Terry would find some other meaningful role in the company; he hoped he could be satisfied working there without moving up the ladder.

Terry was deeply hurt. It wasn't so much that he'd gotten passed up again for the promotion. It was that Ray and the organization had made a fool out of him by not being honest with him until now. If he was in the wrong company, or pursuing the wrong type of work, or if he lacked the right experience and education, then why had he wasted the last few years waiting for a promotion that was never going to come? Terry wished Ray had talked to him honestly a long time ago. That would have helped him move on with his life in a more positive way.

Eye Contact

Relationships: Meaningful Connections or Barriers?

In fact, relationships can be both meaningful connections and barriers – sometimes simultaneously. Relationships can be sources of strength – or complex problems that defy solution. They can give us positive energy and encouragement, or they can de-motivate and de-energize us. But as with so many other aspects of leadership, our relationships are in large part a product of our own intentions and our own thought patterns.

Leaders recognize it may not be within their scope of influence to single-handedly change the company structure, rewrite its budget, or drive corporate strategy. Leaders also know they can't fundamentally change another person's values or behaviors. But leaders hold themselves uniquely accountable for how they show up in their relationships, and for the impact they have on others.

Leaders see all relationships as vehicles to achieving their vision. So they evaluate how their relationships contribute to the gap between their current reality and their vision – and how they might bridge that gap. While others are stymied and frustrated by the barriers that relationships put up, the leader is busy breaking through those barriers, continually and resourcefully building strong and meaningful connections.

The uncompleted conversation, the relationship at odds, the misunderstanding between peers, the failure to challenge mediocrity – these are all components of the gap. For a leader, the leap over the gap is not just strategic – it is a courageous leap into relationship. Like any other leap, this entails risk.

Relationships can flourish even during tough times

Numerous external factors impact a business relationship. Poor departmental leadership, for example, will put stress on every relationship in the department. Rough business conditions can create scarcities that put people at odds with one another. And as we will learn in Plank 9, a lack of shared vision and purpose will also place external stress on any business relationship.

But leaders operate from the belief that these difficulties need not destroy relationships. In fact, the tougher the circumstance, the more the leader will reach out to *connect, with meaning*. Anyone can create harmony in relationships when times are good. When relationships are under duress, the leader invests even more in those relationships to make them whole and productive.

Some business relationships are relationships of necessity. But even when they don't resonate for reasons of personality or "chemistry," every relationship offers opportunity. The leader mines that opportunity, working to realize its potential – by connecting with meaning.

Meaningful Connections

Taking Off Our Masks

People tend to hide from difficulty and conflict. We choose harmony even when it really means superficiality. Yes, harmony that results from failure to talk about what's important isn't really harmony at all. Instead, it's passive, fear-based acceptance of mediocrity.

Consciously or unconsciously, we calculate the potential cost of addressing sensitive issues with others, and compare it to the costs of leaving the issue unresolved or maintaining the status quo. All too often, out of fear, we decide against pursuing the deeper connection or the breakthrough dialog. We don't leap the gap to reach a vision of powerful and fulfilled relationships.

Of course, it's often our own insecurity that makes us shy away from talking about important things. If we think we're likely to be shot down, we take the safer route. We may not trust ourselves to handle the anger or emotion (ours or the other's) that can result from a sensitive conversation.

Insecurity stunts the growth of relationships in compounded ways. The very behavior that results from our insecurity – the failure to enter courageously into conversations and relationships – feeds our insecurity and makes it an even more dramatic barrier. Because we fail to address what's most important in our relationships, they become more and more problematic and complex, and our insecurity grows.

It's critical, then, to confront insecurity and muster the courage to speak to the heart of issues with others. Like any other behavior, the courageous leap into meaningful relationships – relationships that provide paths forward for both people – needs to be practiced.

In her groundbreaking book *Fierce Conversations,* Susan Scott notes that "relationships succeed or fail one conversation at a time." In fact, she adds even more succinctly, "the conversation is the relationship." Scott powerfully challenges us to think of the quality of our relationships in terms of our ability to talk about what really needs to be talked about. Without this capacity to engage in what she calls "fierce" conversations – meaning not violent or mean, but intensely purposeful – we will fail to realize the potential of our relationships. *Fierce Conversations* also gives excellent guidance for preparing for and engaging in these conversations.

Once you believe that "the conversation is the relationship," you will be fundamentally dissatisfied with superficiality and "masks" in the important relationships in your life. So the first step on the path to great relationships is to confront your own insecurity and build the capacity to drive connections of meaning.

The Qualities of Meaningful Connections

Relationships that work in the business world have attributes of strength and of sensitivity. Of course, sensitivity itself can be described as a form of emotional strength. We can define strength and sensitivity respectively as the "backbone" and "heart" of our relationships.

The Five Roles That Create Backbone In A Relationship

Visonary Leader

Relationships need a visionary foundation just as surely as do organizations. In any key relationship, both partners should have a strong, clear sense of the potential of the alliance.

Few of us look at our relationships in this manner, but what a difference it makes when we do. When you establish a vision and goals for a relationship, it stimulates cooperation, creativity, and challenge. We tend to think of vision as something "out there" – a broad statement relating to big-picture issues. But vision can be made very local and very concrete between two people.

You can propel any relationship to the next level by asking, "Why are we here? What can we achieve together that we can't achieve alone? How can we help one another succeed?" Questions like these can launch and sustain a partnership, an entire career, even a great company.

Truth Teller

Every leader – in fact every person – needs truth tellers in their lives and careers. Your truth tellers will share insights about you and your effectiveness that no one else will. These truths, when offered with care and sensitivity, cannot be ignored in a meaningfully connected relationship.

What kinds of challenging but powerful messages might your truth teller deliver? That you are extending yourself too far, for example, or that you have unwittingly alienated members of the team, or that your work on a project is below your capabilities. Truth telling, like so many other attributes of meaningfully connected interaction, can put relationships at risk. But relationships that avoid the truth will never realize their potential for greatness.

Noble Adversary

Great business relationships depend on the ability – even the invitation – to disagree with nobility, and, when necessary, to agree to disagree. These qualities are essential to the growth of both individuals and organizations. When leaders find that no one disagrees with them or offers alternative views, they should take this not as a validation of their brilliant powers of insight and persuasion but rather as a failure of their relationships.

The role of adversary can of course be overplayed. Some people just enjoy being contrary. But the truly noble adversary makes you stronger, intellectually and emotionally. If you never have to articulate and defend your opinions and ideas, they will lack clarity and strength.

It's best to cultivate noble adversaries among those you trust. Better to have your ideas challenged early on by someone with whom you have a meaningfully connected relationship than later by a senior executive or a client during a presentation.

Challenger

The best relationships offer healthy, positive challenges to all parties. Most of us meet the basic standards set for us in the workplace, but it fuels our growth, our confidence, and our competence when someone points us toward higher achievements or helps us think creatively in pursuit of goals and dreams.

Again, the leader's impulse to challenge others may put some relationships at risk. Some people need constant validation and reassurance; they may want nothing else from their leader. But the leader needs relationships that challenge. If those relationships can't be found within the team or organization, the leader will seek them elsewhere. Leaders are fundamentally dissatisfied with relationships that foster mediocrity. In a generally healthy relationship, the leader will respond to challenge in a healthy way while offering similarly constructive challenges to others.

Moral Voice

How many people have strayed down an unethical path for want of a friend who would call them back to the high ground? Behavior that is dishonest, hurtful, or at odds with organizational values should be challenged. Our strongest business relationships must have a moral grounding. Peer pressure is extremely powerful, because our behavior is often dependent on the cultural context. When we interact with people who think it's okay to fudge the expense account or create phantom invoices in order to meet the monthly target, or collude with competitors on prices, we are more likely to behave accordingly – no matter how well grounded we are individually. We need relationships that give us the courage to resist temptation.

To evaluate the moral fiber of a relationship, ask, "Am I a better person – have my character and values been elevated – by knowing this person?" If the answer is no, the relationship has failed to bring out your best and probably lacks a meaningful connection.

The backbone of a relationship is what makes us proud to partner with the other. The five roles defined above generate growth, achievement and character. But relationships also need a sensitivity of heart to complement the powerfully challenging foundation of backbone.

> **Making It Real**
> *Evaluate Your Relationships*
>
> Choose a colleague or an employee with whom your business relationship is not ideal. Use the *Path Forward Relationship Evaluator* (see Appendix B, page 233) to assess the real nature of your relationship – to clarify misunderstandings and barriers in the relationship. Then create a set of specific intentions for how you will enhance these scores – in other words, what actions you will take to influence the relationship in positive ways. Add time frames for these action steps, and create a structure for holding yourself accountable for making good on them.
>
> Follow up in a few weeks or so to evaluate your progress towards a more productive relationship.

The Five Roles That Create Heart In A Relationship

Understanding Friend

While we are being challenged to do our best, we also need to be deeply understood – we need relationships that support us when we are not our best. Understanding isn't the same as enabling. It doesn't mean we approve of or dismiss the consequences of poor performance or behavior, but rather that we strive to understand the causes and to help the other learn from the experience.

In the embrace of an understanding friendship, we are more likely to own up to our actions and hold ourselves accountable. People who strive to find blame rather than understanding can subvert learning by encouraging others to find excuses and scapegoats, rather than causes and solutions.

Patient Mentor

Inside the heart of a great relationship is the mutual desire to facilitate each other's growth. Impatience and disapproval kills many business relationships. Our patience for helping others learn must of course have limits, but when we take time to apply our insight or experience to guide a person through a challenging situation, we create a deep well of appreciation and trust.

Encouraging Partner

Sometimes we need our relationships to encourage and motivate us when we are struggling. Sometimes events erode our confidence and we simply need to be reminded of our worth and our capabilities.

And sometimes the strongest leaders get the least encouragement. Remember that the word "encourage" literally means to help to find courage or confidence. The wise leader knows when a supportive word or a pep talk is helpful and appropriate.

Trusted Associate

Our relationships stand or fall on the critical foundation of trust. When trust is damaged – when a confidentiality is broken, or a commitment abrogated – the heart of the relationship is damaged along with it. All too often, that damage spirals downward into conflict and unhealthy self-protection.

Understanding how trust is forged and eroded in relationships is a special realm of leadership insight.

Forgiver

Sometimes forgiveness is difficult. But this most evolved of human character traits – the capacity to forgive – is also a strong leadership trait. The leader understands that business is a human endeavor and therefore imperfect. People make mistakes. But when grudges over those mistakes are being nourished, healthy relationships and productivity are not. Forgiveness often serves not just the soul but the health of the team and the business.

It's not helpful to emphasize being right or to punish others for being wrong. Soon enough, we too will be wrong about something. How can we expect forgiveness from others if we have not offered it to them in the past? Rather than holding on to blame or self-righteousness, the forgiving leader seeks out the lessons embedded in mistakes.

Relationship Barriers

People issues are often the most difficult barriers to overcome. They must be approached with sensitivity, creativity, and determination. Too many of us cave in when facing relationship barriers. We can't always overcome them in the workplace, but the leader who wants to drive growth in his relationships and his organization will strive to see these barriers as opportunities.

Communication Barriers

Poor communication is most often cited as the single biggest source of dissatisfaction in organizations. Reasons for poor communication can be emotional, cultural, or institutional.

A leader chooses to model constructive communication, even when others do not. A leader goes out of her way to communicate, even with others who don't communicate well in return.

Sometimes the leader has to find new and different ways to communicate, while striving to understand others' communication styles. Sometimes the leader has to nag people to keep information, ideas, concerns, and insights moving through the organization. The leader asks a lot of direct questions to draw thoughts out. The leader understands that many people don't naturally communicate voluntarily or routinely, so she strives to create an environment where communication is given consistent encouragement and proper channels.

Production Barriers

Often the slow or incomplete work of one individual or team causes problems for others. An individual can become a production barrier by choosing other priorities, by being bureaucratic, by procrastinating, by being perfectionistic, or by not asking for help when they fall behind.

When your own productivity is held hostage by another, you tend to consider it out of your control, especially if it's under the management of a peer or another manager. The leader doesn't simply accept delays, but works to mitigate them, in several ways:

- First of all, the organization needs to understand the costs of production delays. This doesn't mean you grandstand with statistics to shame someone into changing their behavior. It means you dispassionately share information about the cost to the company.

- Secondly, the leader offers help. Though you might perceive someone else's behavior as foot-dragging, the production barrier may have a valid explanation – conflicting priorities, poor processes, or a barrier further up the line. As a leader, your goal is to solve the problem at its root. This may mean you have to confront another person or team in the organization. If you connect with meaning – if you confront them with facts, with an offer of help, and with the best interests of the organization at heart – you will often be successful at breaking production log-jams.

Triangulation Barriers (Passive Aggressive Barriers)

The urge to discuss problems or issues with third parties is at the core of many troubled relationships. We sometimes do this because it is easier to complain about a person to a third party than to have a tough conversation.

Leaders do not engage in this kind of "triangulation." When confronted with evidence of triangulation from others ("Guess what Bob said about you the other day?"), the leader doesn't work his way back through the triangle but instead goes directly to the source. Leaders encourage direct communication as a norm in the organization. They do this by modeling professional, respectful, and honest dialog and by challenging behavior in themselves or others that creates triangulation or passive attack.

> **Making It Real**
> *Repair a Communication Triangle*
>
> *Eliminate a triangle.* Carefully review all your work relationships: Is there any situation at work that you are dealing with indirectly, by using a third party to intercede, or by communicating with a third party inappropriately or ineffectively? Create a breakthrough by eliminating the third leg of the triangle and going directly to the source.

Trust Barriers

Trust is the most critical quality in communication. Trust can break down when competence is in question, when people don't follow through on commitments, or when integrity is violated.

A loss of trust can shut down relationships – permanently. The effective leader confronts trust issues head on and works to build trust back. He acknowledges what has happened, identifies how trust was lost, and invites both parties' perspectives and emotions around what happened. He does this both when he has lost trust in someone else and when his own behavior has created an erosion of trust. Leaders take full accountability; they work to restore damaged relationships back to health.

There are of course other barriers to meaningful connection – for example, unhealthy competition, violations of organizational values, perceptions of unfairness, and inconsistency in the application of policies and procedures.

But regardless of the source of the barrier, leaders are seldom simple victims of the actions of others. At the very least they are *thoughtful* victims, seeking to understand the situation and planning mature and positive responses. And while the barriers that others erect may hurt them, they never take the low road of blaming or using the failures of others as an excuse to avoid accountability for their own choices and actions.

Holding ourselves accountable for the success of our relationships isn't easy. It means suspending harsh judgments of others and working to make meaningful connections even when these connections don't come easily or naturally.

Making Meaningful Connections

When we connect with meaning, the potential positive outcomes are limitless. Most notably:

We grow. Meaningfully connected relationships are primary drivers of our growth and maturation process.

We understand. In the context of great relationships, we gain deep insight. When we come to understand how meaning is exchanged in these relationships, we become more powerful and inspirational leaders.

We are inspired. By learning the stories, motivations, and worldviews of others, we are inspired to reach our potential. When we reach the end of our careers, we will probably measure our success not by the number of widgets we produced, but by the quality of the connections we made with others on the journey.

We are challenged. Leaders see relationships as the engine that drives performance – ours and others. We set our personal standards higher in the presence of those who challenge us. Leaders constantly seek to challenge and be challenged.

What if we have exhausted the possibilities?

Even the most mature leader will encounter individuals with whom they cannot forge a meaningful connection. This may result from a lack of maturity or integrity on the part of the other, or a significant difference of philosophy or vision. When our best effort to create a meaningful connection doesn't work, both parties have choices to make. The relationship may best be ended rather than tolerated.

In relationships, as in all matters of business, we must consistently maintain a difficult balance: while we hold ourselves accountable, we also must hold others accountable. Sometimes problems occur that we didn't create or cannot solve. But if our relationships are built on the platform of our own self-leadership, we can more easily decide when we have done what we can and can do no more.

Fortunately, the hopelessly dysfunctional relationship is rare, and thus should rarely be the focus of the leader's attention. In general, the leader seeks and finds a treasure chest of potential in the people around her. Meaningful connections are the way to unearth and develop that potential.

Plank 8

Leadership Language

Communication overlays every aspect of leadership

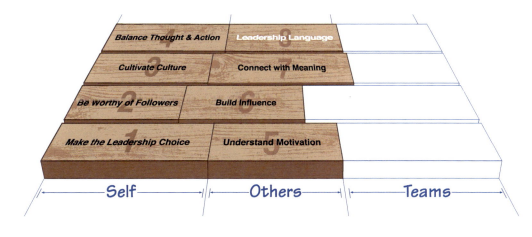

Beatrice, the newly appointed manager of Accounts Payable, had come to Exact Medical Supply from a competitor. After a few weeks on the job, Beatrice discovered a critical issue she needed to take to her boss. She knew this would be an early and important test of her ability to work effectively in her new role.

Dave, Beatrice's boss, was Assistant Controller. Despite his busy schedule, he'd so far been cordial and helpful. He'd introduced Beatrice to everyone in the department, made sure her new-employee paperwork was taken care of, and checked in regularly to make sure she was doing all right. The honeymoon was going well, so Beatrice felt safe to test the waters by bringing a potentially conflictive situation to him.

Recently, Accounts Payable had made a number of late payments to a key supplier. AP was required to have certain forms in place before issuing checks, but the Receiving Department was processing this paperwork in a shoddy way. If Beatrice was going to make the payments on time, the performance of the Receiving Department would need to improve.

Meanwhile, Beatrice and her department were taking hits from sales, marketing, and other managers for "creating" this issue with their largest supplier. There was widespread concern that the relationship between Exact Medical and this supplier was deteriorating, leading to possible disruption of shipments.

Beatrice was too much of a professional to publicly lay the problem at someone else's doorstep, so when complaints came her way she always offered to look into them and try to solve the problem. She'd made several polite inquiries to Receiving, but so far nothing had changed. Uncertain of her authority, and in need of help, she had decided to talk to Dave.

> "I'll take care of it tomorrow. Don't you worry." With that, he dashed out the door, leaving Beatrice wondering what "take care of it" meant.

When she told Dave she had something important to talk to him about, he scoffed and said, "Doesn't everybody?" But he agreed to meet with her "later in the afternoon" and asked her to come by his office. So she did – 3 times. Each time, he waved her off, too busy to engage with her. Finally, at 5:05, she saw him putting his jacket on and leaving his office. She dashed to his side and accompanied him down the aisle.

"Dave, we've been making late payments to Grandel Manufacturing for several months now. Were you aware of that?"

Dave continued walking. He waved at a colleague across the hall and made a brief comment about the upcoming football game. Beatrice waited patiently but began to get a sinking feeling about the encounter.

Finally Dave, turning his attention to his BlackBerry, said, "Yeah, I heard there's a problem there. I thought we hired you to solve these things...." His voice trailed off as he neared the front door – as if the conversation were over.

Beatrice continued to press, believing that might be what it took to get an issue in front of Dave. "The problem is we are getting slow paperwork from Receiving, and I'm not sure what to do about that. It might be a process or IT problem, or they might be just too busy down there. What do you suggest I do?"

Without turning back to look at Beatrice, Dave said, "I'll take care of it tomorrow. Don't you worry." With that, he dashed out the door, leaving Beatrice wondering what "take care of it" meant.

She found out, much to her displeasure, the next day. During a meeting with her staff, Dave barged in and announced with a smile that he had "straightened things out" with Receiving – the late paperwork "won't be a problem anymore."

Beatrice was embarrassed and disturbed. Dave had clearly misunderstood her request for advice as a call for him to use his hierarchical authority to call someone out on her behalf. His actions caused Beatrice to be distrusted by her own staff, who now wondered if it was her style to solve problems this way. And the next time she walked into the Receiving Department, she could only guess at the response she'd get.

Not only did Dave not listen effectively, he also took action without informing Beatrice of his plans. He didn't focus on her or her needs. He made it difficult for her to get time with him. As a result, his relationship with Beatrice was damaged. To make it even worse, he thought he'd done well – and patted himself on the back for his triumphant problem-solving announcement and for what a good boss he'd been.

Turn on the Lights

In consulting with and training leaders, I often play the role of observer. I'm consistently surprised how easy it is to discern the quality of communication in an organization by observing attitudes, demeanor, and interactions there.

In organizations with excellent communication, I see a relaxed, purposeful, and productive flow. In organizations with poor communication, I see frustration, tension, and a stream of perpetual crises that put people on the edge and degrade their work experience, their motivation, and their sense of self-worth.

The difference between these two levels of communication is dramatic and immediately observable. It affects every facet of the employee and customer experience. Healthy, open communication is essential to success, underlying every aspect of leadership.

Let's look back through the planks we've built so far and discuss how communication is central to all of them:

Plank 1 - Make the Leadership Choice
There's not much value in being a visionary if you don't have the commitment, energy, or skill to connect with others and communicate your vision. You can't achieve your goals if you can't communicate your commitment and excitement around them.

Plank 2 - Be Worthy of Followers
Most of the qualities that help you attract followers are communication-based. Every day you experience hundreds of touch points with other people. An effective moment of communication in each – whether through words, gestures, or just listening – creates positive ripples.

Plank 3 - Cultivate Culture
An organization's culture is revealed and reflected in its communication. Culture is taught, reinforced, and propagated through communication. Likewise, the ability of an organization to grow and adapt is directly tied to the effectiveness of communication from leadership.

Plank 4 - Balance Thought and Action
To manage our time effectively and create "sandal" time, we must communicate our intentions and priorities effectively.

Plank 5 - Understand Motivation
To create a motivating environment, we must be good listeners, and we must be able to translate company vision and values into messages that resonate with each individual.

Plank 6 - Build Influence
The ability to influence others is fundamentally the art of communication, especially the art of listening.

Plank 7 - Connect with Meaning
How connected do you feel in your relationships at work? It depends on your ability to communicate effectively – and on the level of trust present. We have repeatedly brought up the importance of trust in building the platform. Communication skills are a prerequisite for building trust.

So we come to Plank 8 with the clear understanding that communication underlies every aspect of leadership and management.

If you think about your daily activities, it's easy to see how the effectiveness of everything you do is determined by your ability to communicate:

- setting expectations and holding people accountable
- giving instructions and providing coaching
- problem solving
- planning and goal setting
- customer and supplier relationships
- recruitment and hiring

What is Leadership Language?

- setting the stage, mentally, physically, and emotionally, for good dialog
- listening with commitment, skill, focus, and an open mind
- processing what we've heard with a curious and unbiased approach
- facilitating intelligent dialog by posing challenging questions and inviting input
- generating productivity through clarity in expectations and priorities, and by consistently providing the context of vision and strategy

Leadership Language creates:

- safety and trust
- sustainable motivation
- effective conflict resolution and problem solving
- personal regard and loyalty toward you
- higher levels of employee cognition and awareness
- healthy accountability

The experience of employees in your organization will be largely determined by how well you communicate with them. If you examine workplace complaints and demotivators, you'll realize many of them are some version of the following statements:

- "My boss doesn't listen to me."
- "Things happen around here and I only find out about them after it's too late to do anything."
- "It's like no one even knows I'm here."
- "I'm always told what to do but rarely why or even how."
- "I don't know how decisions are made in this company."
- "Whenever I try to bring up an issue with my boss, she's on the phone or checking emails. I feel like the last thing on her priority list."
- "I feel like a mushroom – kept in the dark and fed fertilizer."

Running an organization with poor communication is like asking employees to work in the dark. Effective communication "turns on the lights" and enables productivity.

Two-thirds or more of a leader's day is spent in communication with others – conversation, facilitation, or written correspondence. So if you want to become a better leader, it only makes sense to focus your skill development on what you spend most of your day doing.

Reading this chapter will, of course, not be enough. There are many good books on the subject and great seminars to attend. Self-assessments and 360's can also be very helpful. And if you do all that, it's still not enough. Practicing the skills you learn – every day, in every interaction, with humility and commitment – is the road to great leadership.

Consider this chapter an introduction to a very complex subject – an exercise in creating awareness of what's critically important for your leadership development. Practicing will be up to you.

Our model for communication breaks the subject into four components:

Creating the Foundation: Quality communication starts before words are even exchanged.

Input: The art of listening well – of gaining complete and accurate information while making others feel valued and acknowledged.

Processing: The internal dialog that filters your communication through your prejudices, mental models, and assumptions.

Output: The expression of your thoughts, feelings, and decisions, as a reflection (hopefully) of your commitment to developing collective intelligence in the service of results.

The Components of Leadership Communication

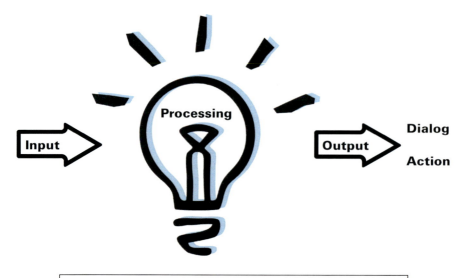

Creating the Foundation

We enter every interaction predisposed by our mental state for either success or failure in that interaction – before any words are exchanged.

Positive Intentions

Your leadership success is a function of your intentions. If you have positive intentions and limited skills, you'll still have an advantage over highly skilled leaders who have dishonest or self-serving intentions. People can see your true intentions; they respond to their perception of those intentions.

So the first rule of good communication is to check your intentions. Ask yourself if you're only looking out for yourself or if you're trying to create a mutual win. Ask yourself if you really want to help the person you'll be interacting with, or if it's your intention instead to scold, correct, or punish – and thus make yourself superior.

The quality of our relationships is determined by the degree to which we accept ourselves and others as being fundamentally "okay" in the interaction. Entering into communication with the preconception that one or both of you needs to be "fixed" will produce an unsatisfying outcome. This can be difficult, especially if recent events have created frustration and conflict. But shifting your mind into positive expectations – expecting a fruitful encounter – changes everything.

Before entering into communication with others, ask yourself "What would be the best outcome of this conversation for both parties?" Then check your behavior and language during that interaction to make sure you're seeking that outcome.

Power Sharing

Conflict and crossed conversational wires can be a result of a perceived imbalance of power. If one partner in an interaction feels overpowered, communication will be diminished. In all communication, especially communication between people at different hierarchical levels, it's important that the intent is to share power.

Your true power comes from your character, your passion, your authenticity, and your talents, not your rank. You do well when you openly share this power and when you are open to experiencing the power of the other.

I once had an unsatisfactory relationship with a boss, and I wasn't sure why. In reflecting on it later, I realized that in every interaction with him, his position above me in the hierarchy was subtly or obviously present – he always found a way to remind me who was boss. Our interactions were cordial and professional, but I didn't feel heard or valued. He didn't share his power with me in ways that made me more effective and powerful. As a result, I felt small in his presence and did not do my best work for him.

At the core of great leadership is an intention to make others more successful and powerful. This doesn't diminish your personal power in any way – in fact, it expands it, because unleashing and sharing your personal power leads to greater results and satisfaction for all. It also makes you attractive and safe for others, and thus sets the stage for effective communication.

Seek Understanding

In Stephen Covey's great book *The 7 Habits of Highly Successful People,* he speaks of the foundational intention to "seek first to understand, and then to be understood."

The intentions to be still and silent, to observe and evaluate, to empathize and understand, are the most powerful intentions for communication. If you enter into every communication with the primary intention of being understood, the other person will likely feel set upon and defensive. Furthermore, you might miss critical information, so seeking first to understand leads to smarter choices and better problem solving.

Even in a conversation where you have important information to deliver, or a corrective message, you can also seek to collect information and develop understanding. What might I have missed in my analysis of the situation? How did the person respond to my message? Did it resonate? What did body language and voice inflection tell me about their state of mind? A leader is a sponge for input and information. By soaking up information you are better able to serve and lead.

The leader's greatest tool is understanding – of people, situations, culture, and of how systems work. This understanding cannot be developed by talking, or by first seeking to persuade or correct.

Create the best environment for the communication

In Plank 2, we talked about the need to be fully present for others, and if that's not possible, to reschedule the interaction for a time when it is possible. This is a fundamental intention of good leadership: to be in the moment, engaged, and focused when communicating with others.

What creates the right environment for positive communication?

- Eliminating distractions. We live in a busy world, a multi-tasking world, a "connected" world. Paradoxically, this emphasis on being "available" to others through technology and open-door policies can make us less available to those in front of us. The idea that people can do more than one thing at a time is more myth than reality, brain research shows. You really can't do two things at once – and if you try, both will suffer. The people you work with want and deserve to be the center of your attention. Doing so will help them feel more valued, and thus more motivated. Furthermore, if you give them your full attention, you'll leave the conversation with better, more accurate information, unfiltered by distractions.

- Choosing private versus public venues. Tough conversations are sometimes needed, but they should never take place in public. If you've ever been chewed out publicly, you know it's an awful experience. Not only is it humiliating and degrading, but the message is often lost because it's impossible to listen well when you're experiencing strong emotions.

- Operating from an equal power base. If you are in a supervisory position, be mindful of how employees perceive being spoken to from the seat of power – your office. Remember that "being called into the boss' office" has negative connotations, so it may be wise to move into a neutral space to create a better environment for dialog. Also, avoid standing physically above others, as being spoken down to can be a physical as well as metaphorical experience. If you have to talk about sensitive issues in your office, come out from behind your desk and sit or stand at eye level with the other person.

- Choosing face-to-face versus written communication. Many managers deliver tough messages in writing. Sometimes this reflects a good intention: to get it right, to think through the words carefully. But too much of the message is lost in writing. Research shows that less than 10% of the content of any message is carried in the words alone; most of the message gets delivered through tone and body language – or metalanguage and paralanguage, as we'll discuss below. Thus resorting to writing alone (this includes email, of course) leaves your message open to incorrect interpretations. Not to mention the implied lack of courage: Receiving a difficult, critical, or alarming message in writing is the equivalent of having someone toss a hand grenade at you and running hard in the opposite direction.

Now that we've set the stage for effective communication, let's talk about the most important aspect of communication.

Receiving Input – the Critical Art of Listening

Think about someone who really listens to you. How does it feel to be listened to in an intense, sincere, and complete way?

In an organizational context, when we are listened to, we feel valued and validated, and as a result we take our work and our role more seriously. Our levels of confidence, trust, and problem-solving rise significantly. We are more likely to think deeply and critically about the work environment if we know that someone will listen to our ideas and our concerns. We are more likely to share information appropriately – for example, to refrain from gossiping and whining – and thus to exercise better judgment.

A multitude of frustrations result from working for a poor listener. Our response can go in several bad directions. We might become passive and withhold our thoughts and our best efforts. We might get louder, shriller, and more explosive in what we say, hoping the extra drama and volume will get us the attention we desire. We might inappropriately share with others concerns that could have been more constructively addressed with our boss.

When we describe people as "great communicators," we are often referring to how articulate, self-confident, and persuasive they are in public speaking. We'd like to challenge you to think differently. The words that come from our lips, our pens, and our keyboards are important, but even more important is our ability to listen carefully and with discernment to others. Good listening leads to wisdom and good judgment. Good talking sometimes leads nowhere at all.

Most of us have never learned to be good listeners. Like any skill, listening requires focus and practice. To start with, it's helpful to think about the obstacles to good listening. For example:

- Poor time management. If you're too busy, or unproductive in general, your stress will cause you to shut off your listening.

- Inability to put aside distractions and focus on the individual.

- Thinking about how we're going to respond before the other person finishes talking. If you process your response too early, you might completely miss the point. Silence is okay, even though most of us are terribly uncomfortable with it.

- Negative judgment of the speaker. If you've already decided the person or the message has no value, you can shut it off like a light switch and miss critical information. Even if you don't like what you're hearing, you have a challenge, an opportunity, and a responsibility to seek to understand.

- Old habits and learned behavior. Think about what you were taught growing up: "keep your problems to yourself," "don't speak unless you're spoken to," "don't be a whiner," etc. If you weren't raised by careful listeners – and most of us weren't – you may have to work harder at changing patterns.

Good listening is a learned skill for most. Practice it! You can get much better at it if you are committed to doing so. One simple way to improve is to reflect back what you think the other has just said: "This is what I heard. How well did I listen?" Remember that what you hear is always filtered through your values, your experience, your beliefs, and your preconceptions. So it's never a good idea to assume that what you heard is exactly what the speaker meant – especially since, as we mentioned earlier, there is a great deal more to language than words.

Paralanguage refers to the physical gestures or energy of the communicator. Examples include crossed legs, waving arms, raised eyebrows, or the presence or lack of eye contact. We're always taking in information from paralanguage, and making assumptions and interpretations. It's crucial to cultivate awareness of these assumptions and interpretations, and to check for accuracy when necessary and appropriate.

We should also watch carefully for incongruities, such as someone saying, "Glad to meet you," with their hands in their pockets and their eyes turned away. Managers often take people at their word, but the attentive listener digs deeper if the paralanguage they see indicates resistance, concern, or discomfort – even if the words sound right. This ability to evaluate non-verbal messages is particularly useful in conducting job interviews.

Metalanguage is another important aspect of communication that transcends the words used. Metalanguage is the inflection, tone, pitch, or emphasis of words and phrases. The same sentence repeated using different metalanguage produces completely different meanings. Try saying, "I appreciate that" with differing tone or emphasis. The meaning can range from sincerity, through dismissiveness, to outright sarcasm.

Paralanguage and metalanguage teach us there is no substitute for face-to-face communication to acquire the critical additional information that comes from being in the physical presence of the other. Technology is a wonderful thing. It enables us to communicate over distance in a short period of time with a lot of people. But communication that relies only on technology is always incomplete.

Lastly, the good listener strives to get the entire message. We tend to absorb an abbreviated version of what's being said to us. "He's angry," "I better apologize," or "She doesn't understand" are variations on these abbreviated messages. Because we are so busy, and because we desire to digest information in ways that are easy and convenient to us, we oversimplify incoming messages. Rather than listening to the full story, we fit what the other is saying into our preconceptions, and thus unfairly make it our story instead of their story.

To reveal the entire message, the good listener asks open-ended questions judiciously.

- "You've just said that you're really angry with Jeff. Can you tell me exactly what it was that happened between the two of you?"

- "Tell me more about the customer's concerns as they were communicated to you."

- "I'm hearing that you feel rushed and stressed. Tell me more about what's causing that."

- "How so?"

- "Why is that?"

Open-ended questions, when asked with concern and sincerity, help the other to clarify their own thoughts and create their own solutions. Good listeners often create an experience in which the initial issue changes or evolves during the conversation. Good listeners are expert at eliciting the "back story" – revealing the root causes and concerns behind the issue that was originally brought to the table.

For example, an initial statement, "I'm pissed off at Harry," can morph into, "I missed the meeting last week because I was sick, and he got handed a project that I wanted for myself." Or, "I really want a raise" can end up as, "You dismissed my idea at a meeting last week and I feel undervalued as a result."

More than the ability to speak well, the ability to listen well will position you for effective leadership. Make a commitment to being a good listener.

Processing: the importance of a wise inner dialog

Do you realize you're constantly communicating with yourself? You are perpetually trying to make sense of everything that's happening, by categorizing things, people, and experiences, by trying to figure out how what's happening will affect you, and by telling yourself stories that allow you to deal with situations in a way that makes sense to you.

The result of this inner conversation has everything to say about the quality of your interpretation of events, intentions, and circumstances. Improving the quality of the inner conversation enhances mental health, wholeness, and maturity. Having a quality inner dialog leads to more effective leadership and a healthier life overall. The wise leader listens to his own inner conversation as attentively and critically as he listens to others.

Here are five things to keep in mind as you strive to create a healthy and productive inner dialog, processing what's being communicated to you in the most effective way possible:

1. Allow information through your initial defenses so it can reach the higher reasoning part of your brain

At the base of the magnificent complexity of the human brain lies the brain of a reptile. It processes input based on primitive impulses, categorizing things as either "okay" or "scary."

When you're operating from fear, anger, or stress, information fails to pass through your primal defenses – the "fight or flight" filter – into the part of your brain where it can be managed and processed rationally.

Sometimes when we act irrationally, we'll look back later and ask, "What was I thinking?" The fact is we probably *weren't* thinking, or at least not at the level we wanted to be thinking. Our brains have a tremendous capacity for reason, but it's sometimes a battle for the reasoning brain to take charge of the primal brain. Learn to recognize when fear, confusion, or other primal urges are making you … stupid.

2. Be curious, not judgmental

The more I learn about leadership, the more value I put on the curious nature of great leaders. Curiosity is the committed, open-minded search for meaning and wisdom.

We are often overtaken by our desire to judge situations and people. When we operate in judgment, our thoughts and words might sound like this:

- "Here we go again."

- "Isn't that just like him to miss the point."
- "She just doesn't get it."
- "This is a really dumb idea."
- "He doesn't know what the heck he's talking about."
- "This guy will never understand."

Whether your judgment is correct is not the issue. The point is that when we judge others, we close the door on possibility and opportunity. For many of us, it's easier, more convenient, and less challenging to our biases and assumptions to make quick judgments than to drive for deeper levels of understanding. And it's these deeper levels of understanding that are fundamental to great leadership.

Because curiosity often takes time, it isn't part of the culture of many businesses. Business people are taught to make quick calls on the fly. This approach makes sense when we're managing, but not when we're leading. Management requires operating within a set of boundaries, processes, and systems. To manage well, we often have to size things up quickly and take action. But leading is about facilitating growth. As leaders, our quick, convenient judgments, often reinforced by years of experience and habit, can be our worst enemies.

Be curious about everything. Move past your convenient habitual judgments into a deeper and more meaningful level of interaction with the world around you. Things are not always as they seem, and certainly not always as you would want them to be. Your curiosity will serve both your relationships and your leadership.

3. Avoid the tendency to quick-fix the problem or dispense easy advice

Our processing is stunted when we see every conversation as a problem to be solved. When we immediately respond to issues with solutions or suggestions, we're often just pulling ideas off the shelf, from an inventory of solution "products" we have previously manufactured or found.

Of course, experience is a great teacher, instructing us what works and doesn't work in particular situations. But there are two problems with a "quick fix" approach.

First, it may stunt our processing of the situation and prevent us from looking for deeper, systemic causes and effects. In pulling the same solution product off the shelf, we may be giving the right solution to the wrong problem.

Secondly, the quick fix also stunts the development of others. If all your boss does is give you answers, he's not challenging you to grow.

4. Think beyond what will affect you

It is human nature to process all input through the question, "How will this affect me?" But as leaders, we want to be in service to others, so this appropriate and natural question results in incomplete processing. What's best for you might not be best for the team or the organization.

5. Engage your higher self

Your higher self is the voice inside you that makes rational, high-integrity decisions. It is the self that acts with civilized and thoughtful regard for the needs of others. It is the self that makes the right choice – the one aligned with our core values, rather than our base desires. It is the self that we would like to be, but often are not.

And when processing the inputs of the world, you always have a choice. Will you let your higher self lead your inner dialog, with care, patience, integrity, and clarity?

When communication enters your brain, it triggers a complex process of evaluation, story-telling, and emotional processing. Tune into this inner dialog. It may be the most important conversation of all.

Output – your words directed at others

So now, and only now, do we discuss the language that comes from you, in spoken or written form, directed toward others.

A good vocabulary and the ability to express oneself clearly and efficiently are critical skills for a leader. But not all leaders have the capacity to be quick on their feet verbally; even the most highly evolved intellects sometimes require time to process information and form their thoughts into effective language.

Again, as with nearly every aspect of leadership, the key is practice. In the 90's when voicemail was coming into widespread use, I found I had a tendency to be, shall we say, random in my messages. After receiving feedback that recipients were using the "Delete" button with relative abandon ("Where is he going with this?") I made an effort to improve the quality of my messages. For a period of months I would play them back before sending, and I'd re-record them if they weren't crisp and clear. With practice, I stopped driving others nuts with long, rambling messages.

All communication – spoken or written, public or private, interrogative or declamatory – improves with practice. Socrates, when asked, "How do you become a more ethical human being?" was said to have responded (in his typical question-with-a-question way), "How do you become a better cobbler?" The obvious answer: you make shoes. You do it. Over and over. Practice.

Different people process language in different ways

Leaders with high levels of verbal skill are often frustrated by the time and effort required to communicate their messages. This is largely because everyone processes information differently. That's why detectives will tell you that no two witnesses at a crime scene will tell the same story in the same way.

This applies to both speed and method of communication. People who don't process at the same speed as you aren't necessarily less intelligent. They may instead possess a different type of intelligence. Whether speaking to individuals, groups, or entire organizations, be aware of how your communication strategy meshes with the receptiveness of your audience.

A few things to keep in mind:

- Give others time to digest complex or difficult messages. And when appropriate, after each complete thought allow space – even just a second or two – for a response, a question, or just to make sure your listeners are with you. Consistent checks for understanding – using both eye contact and direct, open-ended questions (e.g. "What questions do you have?" or "Tell me what you're not clear on so far") – are critical.

- Be ready to repeat yourself. We often need to hear a new concept several times before we fully understand or embrace it. As we said earlier, it's not enough for a leader to say, "I told them!" and then assume the communication is complete. Make sure people have absorbed the message you're trying to deliver. If you aren't certain, keep trying until you are.

- Use a variety of communication channels. If you've just had a critical conversation or made a critical presentation, follow it up with a written summary. If you've first used written communication, follow up with a conversation to make sure the message was received properly.

- Don't just use words. When face-to-face, use appropriate gestures for reinforcement. And of course good leaders are skilled at using symbols, graphs, and visual aids to get their ideas across.

Own your message!

Every message has two parts – the delivery and the reception. So neither the speaker nor the listener bears total responsibility for the quality of the communication. Each can only take responsibility – and in fact, must take responsibility – for his or her part. On the delivery side, there's a subtle difference between language that exhibits ownership and language that doesn't.

- "I don't understand," rather than "You're not making sense."
- "This is what I need," rather than "It would be nice if…"
- "I've observed that…" rather than "You always…"
- "I want to see a more complete effort from you on this project," rather than "You really should give this project a better effort."

What's the difference between these two approaches to language?

Owning your messages creates more clarity and certainty – in your own mind and in others – about what you want and need. What the leader wants, needs, and observes is important to others. Being willing to put your personal stamp on your message helps others know exactly where you're coming from.

Also, using "I" statements sends the message that you realize your perspective is only one of many; others may differ. You can only make assessments based on what you've observed. This helps create a positive culture of accountability.

Different communication needs require different styles and skills

Your communication will be more effective if you consider the type of communication the situation demands, and adjust your language accordingly:

Language that generates collective learning

Leaders create a learning culture – or not – by how they use language. Some business people have only one approach: "the answer guy." But as we said earlier, simply providing answers doesn't develop quality dialog, doesn't tap into collective wisdom, doesn't promote growth, and thus in the long-term is a competitive disadvantage.

Effective leaders slow down, ask questions, challenge assumptions, and create open-ended dialog to snap others out of tactical mode and into higher planes of thinking.

The language of learning is the language of:

- curiosity ("Tell me more.")
- openness to new possibilities ("What if…?")
- challenging the status quo ("How can we change our thinking about this?" "What isn't working about the way we're currently doing it?")

Good leaders recognize the difference between an immediate tactical need and an opportunity to challenge the organization to break free from routine. This only happens when you create an environment of curiosity and intellectual exploration rather than just providing answers.

Language that generates personal growth

Leaders are skillful at coaching and mentoring others. The language used in a coaching approach is different from instructing or directing.

The language of personal growth is the language of:

- observation
- alternative perspective
- possibility
- encouragement
- accountability

A different language is used when assessing individual performance. Evaluative messages must be honest and direct – keeping in mind that it's not helpful to put someone on the defensive, and it's always beneficial to be encouraging.

Language that generates action

Many managers are fond of pointing out how their employees failed to produce or to follow instructions. If you believe that people generally want to perform well rather than poorly (and I hope you do), then you understand that a negative result can often be traced back to a problem in communication. Again, communication always has two parts. You can't control how your message is being interpreted, but you can deliver your information so as to maximize the possibility of turning on the lights so the work can be done.

Most of us are not nearly as clear with others as we are in our own minds. Too often, employees are not given the proper information or clear enough direction to do the work – and then are blamed for poor results. It is essential for leaders to use language that effectively fosters action.

The language of action is the language of:

- **Context**: What's the vision? Why is the work important? What role does my work play in the bigger picture? What goals are we striving for and what will it mean to achieve them?

- **Expectations**: What will success look like? Specifically what outcome is needed or expected?

- **Priorities**: How important is this work relative to other work that's needed? If I have to make choices about time or resources, how do I decide what gets top priority?

- **Process**: How is the work to be conducted? What are the roles and responsibilities of each person involved? How long should it take and how much should it cost?

- **Follow up**: When will we communicate again to track progress? What types of issues should be brought to the leader's attention as the work progresses?

- **Accountability**: What are the consequences, good or bad, intended or unintended, of the work? Who is ultimately responsible? What's at stake?

- **Appreciation:** If you want employees who care about their work, you'll appreciate that they desperately want to know how they're doing. When they're doing well, they deserve to hear about it – frequently.

Leaders get things done by communicating clearly, consistently, and repetitively about what's important. It's amazing what people can do when they know exactly what's expected of them and feel encouraged and empowered to do it. In his seminal leadership book *The Fifth Discipline,* Peter Senge writes, "The truly committed can accomplish the seemingly impossible." As a leader, your language can fuel – or erode – that commitment.

What we've done in this chapter is scratch the surface. Communication is far too complex and important a subject to cover in depth in a few pages. For your next steps:

- Read further. Great books on leadership abound, fleshing out every plank in the Platform. Ask for recommendations from leaders you admire.

- Regularly invite others to give you honest feedback on your listening skills.

- Join a Toastmasters organization if you want to learn to speak in public effectively. Practice every day and get feedback from people around you on how you're doing. Listen to yourself talking to others, as if from outside of you, and monitor your own effectiveness.

- Focus on setting the stage, being a great listener, and listening to and guiding the "inner" conversation.

Nothing distinguishes a great leader like the ability to communicate effectively. Your commitment to good communication mirrors your commitment to being in service to others, creating winning performance, and developing lifelong relationships of mutual trust and regard.

Making It Real
Understanding Leadership Language

Observe a conversation of more than 60 seconds between two people in your organization. Note as much as you can about the conversation:

- How solid was the conversation's foundation, in terms of the underlying intention to share power, to seek understanding, and to create an appropriate environment?

- Describe the quality of the listening skills you observed.

- What did the body language, voice inflection, and modulation tell you about the messages being conveyed beneath the language? Were these things consistent with the words spoken?

- Was anything resolved? Was action agreed to? Were follow-up procedures established?

- What was your general perception of the quality of the communication that took place?

Based on what you learned from this observation/reflection, what changes will you make in your communication style? How will you help yourself remember to make these changes?

Making It Real
Your Personal Leadership Language

Have someone observe a conversation of yours and comment using the criteria outlined in the previous exercise (Making It Real: *Understanding Leadership Language*).

Based on the feedback you receive, what changes will you make in your communication style? How will you help yourself remember to make these changes?

Leadership of Teams

In the first and second sections of the Leadership Platform we nailed down eight planks having to do with leadership of ourselves and leadership of others:

- Make the Leadership Choice (The Leap)
- Be Worthy of Followers (The Ripple Effect)
- Cultivate Culture (Put Down Roots)
- Balance Thought and Action (Boot and Sandal)
- Understand Motivation (Find Buried Treasure)
- Build Influence (Earth and Moon)
- Connect with Meaning (Eye Contact)
- Leadership Language (Turn on the Lights)

You now see the importance of building the Leadership Platform in its entirety. Without a solid foundation of self-leadership, and without the ability to enter into productive, deep, and honest relationships with others, we're not able to move forward and lead groups or organizations. No matter how broad our responsibilities, or how many people report to us, our leadership of ourselves and our leadership within the context of one-to-one relationships is where success starts.

But as you've nailed the first eight planks down, you've become increasingly capable of having impact in your organization, regardless of how many people report to you. Leadership, as we've said before, is not a measure of the organization chart under your name but rather a measure of your effectiveness and your impact. If you've built the first eight planks of the Leadership Platform, you are already leading, and the lives and productivity of those around you are already better as a result.

However, if you're good at what you do, you'll eventually be asked to lead a team of people. And this is a different challenge from being an "organic" leader or a leader without direct reports. The leader of teams is accountable for the activities of others and is responsible for creating a positive return on their compensation. It's a whole new ballgame.

So, the Platform now extends to four additional planks having to do with Leadership of Teams. Through the development of these skills, the Platform increases in size, stability, and strength, allowing more to join you in your journey toward excellence.

By building the first eight planks of the Platform, you have, by your self-awareness, character, personal productivity, and independent thinking, become a visionary and an achiever. You have, by understanding motivation, building your personal influence, connecting positively with people, and communicating with expertise, made yourself a valuable asset and a person who matters to others.

Now you're ready to take on the great challenge that awaits – to bring diverse people together under your supervision to work effectively and harmoniously.

Teams are complex. What seems like it should be simple becomes complicated when the various assumptions, aspirations, and styles of different people are brought into the equation. There are times when leading teams of people is exasperating and confounding. What should be relatively straightforward – a project, the installation of a new process, the communication of a change in strategy – becomes complicated as the activity is engaged by the collective psyche of the team. The leader of teams is constantly aware of this complexity and embraces the possibilities.

It's a marvel to watch an accomplished leader work his magic on a team. The team feels cared for and well informed. They know their roles and their responsibilities. They have a common vision and use a common language. The team's leader is neither micromanaging nor disconnected. The team is constantly examining the way the work is performed, and constantly working together to make the work more effective and productive. The dialog is productive, and problems are resolved quickly and creatively.

How does a team's leader get the team to this level of performance? The next four planks of the Platform should help you understand and prepare for this challenge.

Plank 9 – Create Shared Vision
Any disconnection or discontinuity among a group of people reduces effectiveness and increases the chances of conflict and dysfunction. This plank deals with the role of the leader as the "master electrician" who connects the wires. Connecting the wires means that the team has a strong sense of its purpose and values, and it connects with and supports the goals of others within the team and within other stakeholder groups.

Creating shared vision means that we direct the positive energy of people in the direction that serves the team. We understand the personal perspectives and aspirations of the people in the team, and we create common ground between what individuals want and what the team needs.

Plank 10 – Expect Accountability
Clearly in a team everyone has to pull their weight. In this plank we talk about how accountability works, about how it flows from a "contract" and about how you as the leader set the foundation for an accountability culture.

Many leaders complain about not "getting what they want" from their employers. In Plank 10 we help you understand that establishing an accountability culture is a result of strong leadership and explicit expectations.

Plank 11 – Develop a Process View
A business is a complex engine in which the gears have to mesh effectively. Enlightened leadership means understanding that most people will perform effectively in a strong process environment. Plank 11 is about developing a view of the business that constantly examines results as an output of processes. Through this awareness, the leader finds that many people problems aren't really people problems at all.

Plank 12 – Your Leadership Legacy
In Plank 12 we point you toward your primary responsibility to lead organizational and professional development in your organization. A leader's job is in large part to develop other leaders, and we propose a system in which your organization will develop the leaders it needs. We also speak to the constant learning mode of the leader, and of how you must continue learning every day for the rest of your career.

Plank 9

Create Shared Vision

I help teams perform by directing their energy toward shared goals

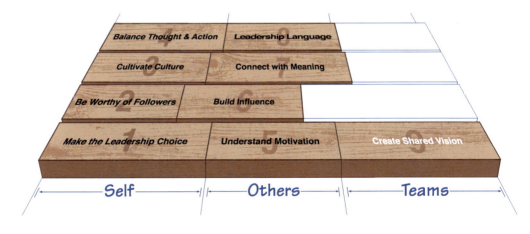

After five years in the purchasing department at Senalent Distribution, Brenda had been promoted to Team Leader.

Brenda had worked hard to develop good relationships with each of her four team members. She'd taken special care to discover each one's needs and understand what motivated them to do their best.

And she'd succeeded admirably. Each member of the team spoke highly of her; each felt a positive impact from her people-focused approach. And they were all performing well.

Recently, Brenda spent a considerable amount of time preparing annual performance evaluations for her team. In doing so, she became aware of a paradox. Whereas she had little negative to say about each team member, she didn't feel nearly as good about the team as a whole. She realized she had fostered individual performance quite well, but she had not done as well fostering cohesiveness or setting and achieving team outcomes.

Maybe this had something to do with Brenda herself. Her style had always been to hold herself highly accountable – to put aside distractions and perform her share of the work to the highest standards. Maybe the team simply followed her lead in this respect. Maybe she had given the impression that hers was to be a group of strong individual contributors, rather than a tightly knit team.

There were symptoms indicating the team wasn't living up to its potential. Team members generally didn't participate in discussions and meetings as much as Brenda would have liked. They tended to go their own way with purchasing processes, justifying their actions by saying "it worked better" that way. Brenda also saw some eye-rolling and frustration when one member asked for help from another. She felt the team members were tolerating one another and not much more.

The first building block of a great team is a vision all the members of the team understand, share, and act upon.

When the time came for Brenda to meet with them individually to review their performance evaluations, she followed the company's formal process to the letter. But she added a question at the end of each review: "What are the two most important things for us to accomplish as a team?"

All four struggled with this question.

Bill replied: "Highest possible inventory turns" and "Acquire product at the lowest possible costs."

Wendy answered: "Maintain an order fill rate of over 95%" and "Keep everyone informed of pending stock outages."

Carl thought: "Find and buy the products with the highest sales potential" and "Negotiate the best possible deals with suppliers."

And Mona said: "Keep from running out of stock" and "Have a fun time at work."

Brenda couldn't argue with any of the eight "most important things" her team had identified. But she couldn't help wondering if there could be more synergy in their views. If Bill was going for highest possible inventory turns, and Wendy wanted a fill rate of 95%, might these goals be incompatible? If Carl was negotiating the toughest deals with suppliers, might those same suppliers be less likely to work with Mona to fill backorders quickly? If Mona wanted to have fun at work, how was that attitude perceived by the others?

Brenda also noticed that some of the goals were concrete and some were not. How would the team know if they were achieving Bill's "highest possible inventory turns" or Carl's "best possible deals"? Goals needed to be concrete enough to create common understanding.

As Brenda looked at the differences among the "most important things," she realized she couldn't expect the members to function as a team unless they aspired to a set of common goals. And these goals would have to be measurable.

Team members need individual motivations and individual perspectives, Brenda realized, but when individuals don't agree on what's most important, opportunities for growth and performance are lost. She started to wonder how she could create common agreement. She looked at the company vision and mission statements for a clue, but they were too general. Maybe her team needed its own vision and mission. She decided to bring them together to start talking out their differences and working toward agreement on common priorities, goals and visions. She didn't know if Bill, Wendy, Carl and Mona could get on the same page, but she needed to give it a shot. Maybe eventually she would give the team the same high marks she was giving the individuals.

Brenda had stumbled upon the most difficult part of building a team. She had proven she could get the most out of individuals. Now she had to maximize their performance as a team.

Connecting the Wires

Even in a team as small as three or four, there is a multitude of possible combinations of people, personalities, agendas, levels of development, maturity and experience. Each task, project, meeting, or hallway conversation creates an ever-shifting mosaic of complex people issues. Every interaction therefore has its own special dynamic, potential, and risk. Each person in the team has their own needs, agendas, and aspirations. The potential for cooperation is immense – as is the potential for disaster.

So we start building the "Leadership of Teams" section of the Platform by asking how we can bring people with diverse needs, expectations, personalities, and abilities together to work productively as a unit.

We begin the discussion by revisiting the concept of vision.

Vision is our imagined future – a compelling set of potential outcomes that inspires our commitment and action, giving us the energy and courage to make "the leadership leap." If we understand how vision can inspire us individually, what might a shared vision do for a team? After all, team effort should be a prime example of synergy – the whole being more than the sum of the parts. But that's only possible if team members are working toward a common end.

A shared vision encourages positive team behaviors and suppresses negative team behaviors. A shared vision makes it less about personalities and more about results. A shared vision helps balance individual needs with the needs of the team, and encourages sensible compromise in the pursuit of team goals. Pursuing team goals can create meaning, camaraderie, accountability, and ultimately, more fun.

So the leader starts building the team by building a shared vision with and for the team. Even before he begins assembling the people, the leader must develop a purpose and identity for the team he wants to create. The first building block of a great team is a vision all the members of the team understand, share, and act upon.

Think about a group of people with whom you have a great deal in common – family, perhaps, or a circle of friends, or an organization. The common ground you feel might consist of values, goals, belief systems, similar senses of humor, or a love of food, a hobby, or a sport.

How do you feel in the presence of these people? You're likely to feel comfortable, confident, accepted, and appreciated. In your social or family environment, you tend to share time and energy based on a cultural connection with others. You have a shared sense of what's important, what's meaningful, and what's fun.

In the workplace we often don't bond with others as easily as we do with friends, family, or common-interest relationships. By its nature, and by necessity, the workplace is more diverse, less built around what we're comfortable with or predisposed toward. So we need to build something around which we can come together in goodwill and common purpose to transcend the natural differences between us. This something is our shared vision.

In the same way that shared vision leads to greater team performance, it also has the benefit of creating teams that are diverse and therefore more dynamic.

Our metaphor of the leader's role in creating shared vision is that of a master electrician. The master electrician locates sources of positive energy, such as vision and motivation, and manufactures wires of communication to foster the flow of commitment and action. The master electrician also makes sure energy is flowing effectively between members of the team, and takes care that it doesn't flow into dead ends – employees who choose not to share or enact the vision.

And if that isn't tricky enough, the master electrician must wire energy between the team and other stakeholders – both within the organization and without.

Stakeholders

Developing an understanding of the concept of "stakeholder" – defined as any entity that has an interest in the team's outcomes – is valuable in developing team identity and cohesion. Identifying all of a team's stakeholders, and then discussing the needs and expectations of each, helps define and broaden the mission and vision of the team.

So who are the people, teams, and business units that have a significant interest in your team's outcomes? And which teams consider you a stakeholder in their outcomes?

Thus shared vision must exist at three levels:

- Personal vision that is congruent with the team vision.

- Team vision that aligns the members with a productive and meaningful role in accomplishing collective priorities.

- A broader vision that informs the team how their behaviors and activities contribute to the achievement of goals and visions of other stakeholders.

The effective leader spends time and energy "connecting the wires" of vision, both personalizing and broadening the vision for each employee. The concept of "win-win," while clichéd, is relevant here. The achievement of team vision is a win for the individual, a win for the team, and a win for the stakeholders. Leaders work hard to connect individual effort and reward to a team focus. In fact, they value efforts and skills that benefit the team more than the individual.

One of the great dilemmas of leadership is this:

When employees are competent (or excellent) individual contributors, how much should I hold them accountable for team-friendly behaviors?

There will be times when an employee can't – or won't – embrace the team's shared vision. He may be uncommunicative, passive, or negative toward others. But he also may simply prefer being an individual contributor. Some of us are introverts – the energy expended in teaming is outside our comfort zone. Some very smart people find their creativity and energy sapped by bringing others along or by compromising on their ideas. Others have never developed team-positive skills – they always got a negative mark on that report-card line: "Plays well with others."

The point is that even a benign, pleasant, and outwardly cooperative person can damage a team if they don't work positively and creatively toward the team vision.

Most managers I've worked with are not sufficiently tuned in to how negative team behaviors offset individual contributions. The leader needs to view the team's performance holistically, as the synergistic product of a joint effort, rather than as the sum of the incremental output of individuals. From this perspective, individuals who contribute "incrementally" without strengthening the team become less valuable in the leader's eyes.

So the critical questions to consider are: Is the solitary person hurting the team? Is there a positive role for her on the fringes of the team, where we can offer a compromise between our need for team-positive behaviors and her need for privacy or independence? Some teams will knowingly support a member who works on the fringe, but this must be by mutual agreement. The team must accept the team-negative behavior as part of their values and norms.

People who choose not to function in a team environment have many opportunities for solitary pursuits in the business world. If an individual's team-negative behavior does more harm than their talent does good, then the leader harms the team by not supporting and challenging them to become more of a team player – or by not encouraging the individual to find a more fitting position elsewhere. Employees who sometimes "do nothing wrong" don't do enough right to be truly productive team members. Leaders act as strong stewards and protectors of their team's vision, encouraging every team member to do the same.

Interdependence

Interdependence is the state of being mutually responsible – for ourselves and to others. We each understand our roles and responsibilities in the team, but we also acknowledge and even honor our dependence on others' contributions to our success.

American culture greatly values individualism and independence. But independence is not the ultimate value. Stressing individual contribution over team responsibility degrades connection and belonging, and makes synergy impossible.

On the other hand, too great an emphasis can be placed on the group. Some cliques, "tribes," or families can subjugate the individual by demanding blind loyalty to the group. This strips the individual of self-determination and individual motivation, creating dependence on belonging and on the ego-identification and perceived safety that derives from it. While we may admire loyalty and cohesiveness, groups can become exclusive, parochial, and ultimately unhealthy. Think gangs.

Interdependence takes the best of both independence and dependence and weaves them into something stronger than either. Great relationships are interdependent – each party brings her best to the relationship, while needing and expecting the best from others. My dual commitment is to my own healthy development and that of the group.

To foster interdependence, we must be mature enough to give up some of our need for individual credit, acknowledgement, and perhaps even short-term financial reward. Leaders teach their employees that contributing to the "commons" produces rewards on many levels – collective and individual.

Office Politics and Interpersonal Conflict

"Office politics" is one of the most common complaints in the workplace. It occurs when individuals advance their own personal agenda in ways that damage the team. Sometimes their intentions are purely self-serving; other times they may be just trying to get things done in an environment that lacks a strong team vision or culture. Office politicians are seen as skillful manipulators of the system, working back-channel relationships to get what they want.

We are quick to criticize this activity, and with good reason. But leaders seek systemic reasons for behavior. What we may not realize is that this behavior is exactly what we should expect when shared vision is absent – or when it is present but there are no consequences for violating the behavioral norms that support the team vision. Office politicians – if they're successful – operate in an environment of failed leadership.

When interpersonal conflict occurs in a team, it too can be due to a lack of leadership. In a team that's purposeless or drifting, individuals can find themselves competing with one another for the attention of management, for praise, for responsibility, or for compensation. People may be confused about their roles or disconnected to the bigger picture, and thus concerned about being blamed or singled out – all of which lead to a feeling of powerlessness. Individuals who feel powerless will sometimes attempt to create power through subterfuge or conflict. Thus conflict within a team may signify a battle for power among disenfranchised or disconnected employees.

Conflict may also quite simply be the result of bad behavior and immaturity – an indication of psychological problems.

Whatever the cause, conflict within the team is a big red flag. Too many managers dismiss it or laugh it off. Courageous leaders who see themselves as stewards of the team's health and vision recognize that a great team must proactively address issues of politics or interpersonal conflict.

Attributes of Shared Vision

Values and Norms
Ideally, values and norms are determined by the team and not for the team. This creates a sense of ownership that is powerfully motivational. It also allows the team to be somewhat self-policing. Leaders encourage regular and open dialog about values and norms. They also encourage team members to nonjudgmentally identify behaviors outside the boundaries they create.

Strategy
How much does your team know about the strategy of the organization they serve? Does your team understand how their efforts serve the bigger picture? When a team understands the context of its contribution, it can create a shared vision that feeds into that bigger picture – giving them motivation to perform more collaboratively and creatively.

Objectives, Goals, and Key Performance Indicators
How is the performance of your team measured? Does every member of the team understand what success looks like? Maintaining a consistent scorecard for your team – an encouraging, rather than punitive scorecard – creates a team focus on outcomes, and thus leads to team-positive behavior.

Process
Is there agreement on how the work is to be performed? Do you share a common conception of the flow of work and the ways in which process is continually improved? Teams can be damaged by independence in process – people doing the same work in significantly different ways. Of course there is always an acceptable level of process variance, and people should be encouraged to brainstorm better ways to perform. But these better ways should then become team ways, not independent variances.

Decision-Making
This is perhaps the most important of all team processes. How do we make decisions? How do team members provide input into the decision-making process? Who will make the decisions? And how will each decision be communicated? The best approach to decision-making is situational. There are times when the team leader makes the call, and other times when a more collaborative or democratic approach is called for. In any case, the decision-making process should be known by all – and it should be as collaborative and transparent as conditions allow.

Roles
Team-negative behaviors can occur quite naturally when roles aren't clear. Interdependence can only exist where we are each clear on our own roles and on the roles of others. This is the foundation for accountability.

Stakeholder Obligations
The team must hold the needs and objectives of the stakeholder community in high regard. Members must take pride in their ability to provide quality work for their stakeholders. This can only occur if the leader raises the line of sight of the team to include the stakeholders. Again, just as we have stressed the interdependence of individuals, we also must stress the interdependence of teams.

Love of the Product and the Customer
A common regard for and pride in the company's products or services is an important component of shared vision. Likewise, a common focus on the customer is essential to shared vision. The desire to excel and to serve others fosters team identity and purpose.

How do we define team-positive behavior?

Shared vision should include clearly articulated agreement on how people will act within the team environment. The list below represents a fraction of what could be included in such a document. You and your team should create your own itemized list.

Team-Positive Behavior	Team-Negative Behavior
Contribute to dialog	Silence
Collaboration	Focus on individual output and concerns
External competitiveness and drive	Unhealthy internal competition; passivity regarding team goals and objectives
Harmony and motivation built from creative tension	False harmony built from avoidance or apathy
Cross-functionality	Silos of competence with little overlap
Participation in continuous, team-driven accountability for improving process	Tolerance of ineffective processes without taking the initiative to drive change
Attention to team goals; personal and shared accountability for helping meet them	Disinterest in team goals and metrics; excuses, blaming; seeing goals and challenges as "someone else's problem."
Positive attitude and encouragement of others	Negative attitude and discouragement of others
Ability to discuss potentially conflictive issues openly with other members of the team	Avoiding conflict, triangulation, and back-door communication
Problem-solving, optimistic approach to change	Complaints; resistance to change

Creating a document like this – as a team exercise rather than flowing it down from on high – can powerfully help bond a team. Once it's finalized, the norms embodied in the document will help hold everyone accountable for team-positive behavior.

Always remember how damaging it is not to follow-up on items you've declared are important. Create consequences for team-negative behaviors – even if the violator is effective as an individual contributor.

> **Making It Real**
> *Understand Your Team's Shared Vision*
>
> How do we assess the extent shared vision is present and active in the team's behavior and interactions?
>
> Make a list of the questions you would ask your team, and your team's stakeholders, in order to learn about the status of the vision shared among them.
>
> Then conduct a survey of your team (and, if appropriate, other stakeholders) to assess *how* shared the team's vision really is.
>
> Based on the results of this survey, schedule actions that will lead to the creation of a more efffective team vision.

The Personal Perspective and the Team Perspective

Teams cannot always satisfy every member's wants and needs. Making decisions by consensus (i.e. unanimously) is ideal. But often individuals need to compromise so the team can move forward.

Leaders work hard to create a complementary relationship between individuals and their teams.

- Make connections with each employee to develop the deepest possible understanding of what they want from their work experience.

- When feasible, explore ways to structure the team and work processes to align each individual's work assignments with his skills, styles, interests, and aspirations. Only impose work rules or schedules when absolutely necessary. What every employee wants is both to be honored as an individual and to feel a sense of belonging to the team.

- Help team members form relationships of understanding and openness. Create time and space for individuals to connect, and encourage them to find the best possible motivations for each other's behavior. Help employees look past petty negative judgments to create an environment of respect. When they have issues with each other, teach them how to air those issues directly, in a tone of curiosity rather than blame.

- Help individuals see the connection between personal achievement and team success. Praise and acknowledge work that benefits the team. Let employees know you care deeply about their personal needs and aspirations and that it's your responsibility to ensure those needs are met in the context of the best interests of the team.

- Don't demand blind loyalty. In many organizations, "team player" is code for "keeps their mouth shut," or "does what I say." Except in cases of emergency, that definition serves the boss's ego, not the team. True leaders seek interdependent team members – people who can express their independent perspectives while caring enough about the team's success to compromise for the sake of the greater good.

Your employees will naturally ask themselves questions like:

- "What's in it for me?"
- "How will this affect me?"
- "How can I get what I need?"

Great team leadership helps each employee also ask these questions:

- "How can I best serve the team's needs?"

- "If I give up something I want, how will the compromise benefit the team and me in the long run?"

- "What needs does the team meet for me (such as camaraderie, tactical support, and encouragement) that would not be met if I weren't part of it?"

Again, we often stress independence to a fault. Sometimes it takes a lot of coaching to help someone put aside their personal ego needs and "fall into" the team, so that we all "play well with others."

We play well with others when we're in a game we're trying to win together. It always strikes me how each fall huge stadiums fill with tens of thousands of people, all rooting avidly for their favorite team. In the pursuit of team vision, we might ask ourselves what brings together this tremendous common energy to support a singular cause. A few of the factors involved:

- A compelling brand, or team identity – promoting a sense of kinship.

- The idea that our ego or personal identity is somehow strengthened through this identity with the team.

- The appeal to the competitive spirit in all of us.

- The fact that winning and losing are so simply identified and measured. The scoreboard tells us clearly whether or not our team is doing well. (And losing teams quickly lose their fans! Who wants to be identified with a loser?)

- The opportunity to identify with talent. On our favorite football team, we enjoy watching people who are faster, stronger, and more courageous than we are – they are our representatives or proxies on the field.

I generally don't like sports analogies, but there are interesting parallels between the spectacle of a football game and a good shared vision. We all know what we're there for – to win (though winning can be defined in more or less healthy ways). We put aside personal differences when we agree on a common identity. We like to keep score. And we like how we feel when we associate ourselves with winners, as long as we get to hold onto our piece of the identity, the glory, and the fun.

And team identity can also be taken too far.

The Foxhole

In war, a foxhole is a dangerous place – a hole in the ground with bullets whizzing overhead. All too often, managers foster a "foxhole" mentality. The foxhole leader tries to convince the team that the world is against them, and the only protection is to huddle together in the foxhole to protect one another from the danger outside.

Teams built by foxhole leaders can be very closed and unified in their culture. They tend to believe they're the good guys, and their success comes despite the incompetence of other stakeholders.

Because this approach can lead to a tantalizing team identity and a strong dependence on the leader to keep the team out of trouble, some leaders either unknowingly or unethically create foxholes for their people – especially in times of stress. Beware of foxholes. If you feel like you and your team are falling into one, come up out of it, into a mindset of interdependence with stakeholders. Even if you have concerns about the support you're getting from your stakeholders, understand that slipping into a victim mentality, or a self-congratulatory "us versus them" stance, is a road to disaster. Like it or not, you live and work in an interdependent world.

Making It Real
Creating Shared Vision

Consider the most notable example of a lack of shared vision that you see – within your team, within your company, or between your team and other stakeholders. What conditions created this situation? How can leadership address it most productively? What, if anything, can you do to remedy this situation, and specifically what action steps are you willing to take in the short term?

In short:

- The foundation of a good team is a shared vision. Create a vision for the kind of team you want. Then when you bring the team together, use your vision as a draft – a prompt to spur creative dialog. Collaborate to form the team's vision, values, and norms. This process ideally includes a broad spectrum of stakeholders.

- Revisit the team's vision, values, and norms on a regular basis. People, circumstances, and dynamics change, and important agreements bear reinforcing. Once is not enough.

- Study and model the concept of interdependence. If your team understands and embraces this concept, it will bond them as a team and encourage team-positive behaviors.

- Work with the team to create a brand, or tribal identity, that encourages them to think of themselves as a team. Remember how keeping score and creating excitement around winning – not defeating, but win-win winning – helps bring diverse people together for a common cause.

- Work closely with team members to integrate their personal goals with those of the team. Remember that individuals naturally bring their own perspectives and will be primarily interested in meeting their own needs until they take ownership of team outcomes.

- Personalize and broaden the vision of the team. The vision needs to be understood at three levels. How does my personal vision fit the team? How does the team vision influence my behavior? What does the team vision say about our collective accountability to all our stakeholders?

- Discourage individual success at the expense of the team. Measure, reward, and encourage team-positive behavior. Think about all your actions as a leader. What messages are you sending through your attention, your rewards systems, your compensation systems, and your choices regarding promotion and work assignments? Are you consistently sending the message that individual accomplishment is only rewarded in the context of team-positive behavior?

- Envision success as broadly as possible. While you are a strong visionary within your team, you are a collaborative visionary, and you work to integrate the vision and goals of your team with those of the entire organization. In other words, the vision for your team must complement and support the visions for all other teams, departments, and units within the business. A disconnection at this level will be felt in the interactions between teams just as surely as a lack of team vision will create conflict between employees.

- Get your ego under control. Great leaders have faith that if they create successful teams, their careers will move forward in the way they want. Great leaders check their ego at the door for the benefit of the team and all its members. They believe that the success of all insures their success. It's called interdependence, and it's the job of the master electrician to connect the wires to make it happen.

Plank 10

Expect Accountability

I balance discipline with freedom and flexibility in achieving results

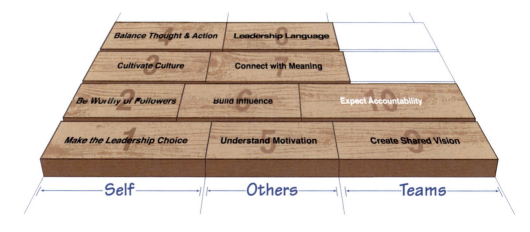

"*I am really worried about my team. They just don't seem to be stepping up. Just yesterday Pam forgot to complete the sales analysis I asked her for, and her only excuse was she didn't have time. Last week at our status meeting, only four of the six steps I wanted done on the reorganization project had been completed.*"

Frank was listening to Roberta, one of his key managers, complain yet again about her team's performance. Roberta was a strong functional employee, focused and organized. It was her high level of productivity that had attracted Frank's attention two years ago when he promoted her to Team Leader. He presumed her ability to produce would transfer to her team.

From the beginning, Roberta had been an enthusiastic manager, quick to praise, with a tendency to trust and empower her employees. And her work ethic was impressive. The team began to improve under her leadership.

But Roberta had hit a wall; improvement stalled less than a year into her tenure. Since then, turnover had increased and quality problems had cropped up.

With her permission, Frank decided to observe Roberta's team closely for a period of a few weeks. He attended team meetings, interviewed several key employees, listened more carefully to the way she communicated, and read between the lines of her emails.

But first he interviewed Roberta. He asked her questions like: How do you hold others accountable for their work? How do you assign tasks? How do you set priorities? How do you respond when things get off track or projects are late?

Roberta told him she believed most of her employees cared about quality and about meeting commitments – but they didn't care as much as she did. This, in her mind, was the problem.

An evolved team with high levels of trust and outstanding communication can begin to create its own accountability without intervention from the boss.

Roberta had trouble with the concept of accountability. She believed it was entirely a personal choice – that if people believed in their commitments and really worked hard, they would meet them consistently. For Roberta, accountability was solely a matter of an employee's will – and good will toward her and toward the company. Accountability problems were, in her view, people problems.

So Roberta was unsure what to do when an employee failed to meet a commitment. She was tentative in her approach, and when she finally worked up the courage to confront the problem, she went into a corrective mode. She gave advice about how to perform the task differently, or simply told them she needed them to do better. It was her hope that by raising the employee's awareness of the deficiency, he would be motivated to perform at a higher level. But invariably the problem would resurface a month or so later, and Roberta would get more and more frustrated.

Frank began to see how Roberta was failing to set the stage for healthy accountability. He noticed that Roberta was cycling through a series of failed new hires, hoping to find ones who would "step up." He saw many things she could do differently, and he began to coach her to make some changes.

For one thing, Frank noticed a lack of specificity in Roberta's requests. Tasks were to be accomplished "when time allowed." When they weren't completed, she would simply ask the employees to "keep at it." Roberta made it clear she wanted things to get done, but she didn't make it clear exactly who was responsible, when the work was expected, and what the consequences were for failure – other than the boss's disapproval, expressed passively or indirectly.

Roberta also didn't talk with her team about their priorities or their challenges. And although she kept a good calendar and a to-do list, she didn't require the same of her staff. So they tended to take a "first-in, first-out" approach rather than making decisions from a strong sense of strategic context or priority.

Instead of discussing logistics, priorities and deadlines, Roberta used sports analogies to point to the importance of determination and competitive spirit. The consistent message was that people got things done because they wanted to – but no attention was paid to whether the system was designed for success.

It was no wonder that her team lacked accountability, Frank began to see.

Furthermore, in the time between meetings, Roberta had a tendency to lose focus on the action steps from the last meeting. Once she assigned a task, she wouldn't follow up. Again, this was largely due to her philosophy of management. "I shouldn't have to follow up with them. After all, I don't have to rely on my boss for follow up." Often this worked, and employees would get the work done. But when they didn't, Roberta was most likely to hear about it from somewhere else in the organization – or worse yet, from a customer.

Roberta, not being process focused, also disdained the use of metrics and analytics to manage her team. With her hands-on approach, she would say that she had a "feel" for when things were going right or wrong. As a result she tended to manage by anecdote, reacting strongly to individual performance failures rather than looking for root systemic causes.

Frank also looked at the way he'd been managing Roberta. She was a workhorse to be sure, self-motivated and consistent in meeting deadlines. But lately he'd noticed her staying later and later to get her work done, and her personal life had suffered the consequences. He'd fallen into the habit of loading her up with work because she never cried uncle. He had always admired her work ethic and her commitment to personal accountability, but now he worried about her burning out. Her focus on "effort" caused her to judge herself harshly when things didn't go right. Her tendency was always to work her way through problems, rather than to be curious, analytical, and non-judgmental.

At the end of his observation period, Frank sat down to discuss his insights with Roberta. "The first thing I've observed, Roberta, is that your strong sense of personal accountability isn't translating into team success. To create true accountability in your team, you need to consider the disciplines of managing your team.

"Expecting everyone to be like you isn't the solution. You need a coordinated approach to organizing your team around the work. They need to know exactly what's expected, and they need to know why the work is important. Their work needs to be measured so that the team is looking at overall results and not at individual incidents. And lastly, they need to stop hearing from you that every failure to perform is a failure of character or work ethic.

"Accountability starts with caring about the outcomes," Frank said, "but it really blossoms when the manager commits to a thoughtful and comprehensive approach."

The Buck Stops Here

Visitors to Harry Truman's Oval Office were greeted by the sign, "The Buck Stops Here." The sign referred to the phrase "pass the buck," which in turn came from the old poker tradition of passing a knife with a buck-horn handle around the table to indicate whose turn it was to deal. "Passing the buck" came to mean avoiding responsibility – passing difficulties to someone else rather than holding oneself accountable for solving the problem.

President Truman's sign signaled his willingness to take on tough issues (which he certainly did) and to stay out of the blame game. It signaled his belief that leadership is, in the end, about results. After all the explanations have been offered, the leader has to be held to account for those results. "The buck stops here" – an important leadership principle – is the substance of this plank.

Of course leaders have the additional challenge of holding others accountable for their behavior and their outcomes. And they have to do it in ways that aren't arbitrary, heavy-handed, or inflexible.

Expecting accountability in your team requires you to balance the need for tangible, specific results with the need to work creatively and collaboratively toward those ends. These may seem contradictory challenges. After all, true accountability requires a certain amount of oversight and binary thinking – either we achieved our goals, or we didn't. In Plank 1, we discussed the dangers of rationalizing failure. But many leaders who claim to be "all about results" take this black-or-white thinking too far, becoming all about control and compliance.

The real challenge of expecting accountability is creating discipline around results while encouraging freedom, flexibility and creativity in how those results are achieved.

We've all worked for the "hard" boss who demands results and doesn't accept excuses. What we learn from this leader is consistency and discipline. We've also worked for the "soft" boss who nurtures relationships, is always open to suggestion, and strives for high levels of personal satisfaction for all team members. What we learn from this leader is the importance of good intentions, empathy, connection, and service to the needs of one's employees.

We need to merge these two personalities in order to create the highest levels of accountability in our teams. It's a balancing act: demanding results while patiently and diligently developing the people and systems that create those results.

The word "accountability" comes from the same root as "to count" or "to calculate." Holding others accountable means we require them to give account of their actions, to "stand up and be counted," so to speak. "Responsibility" shares the same meaning, and adds the implication that accountability should not just be about doing the thing requested, but about doing the right thing.

So accountability can be assessed on two levels: the tactical level and the ethical level. Strong organizations led by strong leaders always address these levels simultaneously. They never become such slaves to results that they compromise their moral responsibility to their teams, their stakeholders, and the world in which they operate.

We were all guilty, as children, of standing next to the broken lamp and saying, "I didn't do it" – even though our parents and the rest of the world knew we did. And, like it or not, our "inner child" – afraid of being exposed, afraid of consequences

– never completely disappears. To see this inner child in action, watch the evening news – full of dysfunctional people who, with the microphone in their face and the cameras rolling, give outrageous explanations for their bad behavior.

We all have this natural tendency to avoid responsibility and thus, as we've discussed, find extrinsic causes for our failures. Rationalizing is about avoiding the inner-child pain of accountability for poor results.

Of course fear is at the source of it all, even for us adults. It is sometimes rooted in legitimate lower-level needs: losing one's job, or being passed over for promotion. Sometimes it's fear of being revealed as incompetent, or of being judged harshly by others. The resistance to accountability can be so strong we begin to believe the stories we've made up to protect our egos.

So since fear erodes accountability – not to mention trust and productivity – part of the leader's job is to reduce fear. I also said the leader's job is to foster freedom and creativity within a disciplined context. The tips and strategies in this chapter – and, to a large extent, throughout this book – address both those critical leadership responsibilities.

Developing accountability in teams starts, of course, with the leader. You must manage it in your everyday activities. You will have strong inner voices that will want to explain away or ignore negative consequences. Find the inner voice that says, "The buck stops here." Listen to it above all others.

Team Accountability

Even though the leader is ultimately responsible, an evolved team with high levels of trust and communication will maintain its own accountability without much intervention from the boss. This is an inspiring goal – to create team dynamics that produce a culture of mutual interdependence and accountability.

But developing such a culture is always a work in progress. In the beginning stages, some leaders often find themselves checking in, reminding, even nagging. Especially when taking over a team that hasn't developed that culture of mutual accountability, the leader may have to be very hands-on. But overly close supervision will only be necessary over the long run if the leader himself is undisciplined. Once the leader establishes a consistent pattern of clear expectation and disciplined follow-up, nagging ceases to be necessary – fortunately, since no one likes to be micro-managed.

Setting the Foundation

As with the challenge of good communication, if you expect accountability you must build the foundation on which it will flourish. This foundation is composed of values, vision, discipline, a healthy learning environment, and solid leadership character.

Values and Vision

Here we encounter one more example of the power of a values-driven approach to leadership. A values-focused team is more likely to develop a strong sense of mutual accountability – especially when the stated values *include* mutual accountability.

When leaders and employees agree on values, discuss them regularly, and integrate them consistently, trust also develops. And trust, in turn, helps team members want to be mutually accountable – not to mention more competent, creative, and cooperative.

So to foster a high level of accountability for the work, the leader fosters accountability to the team's values. I would suggest these values reflect a strong focus on both interdependence and personal responsibility.

A powerful vision also tends to unite the team – not only because everyone's working toward the same goals, but also because they're more likely to avoid conflict and support each other in their quest to reach them. The lack of a unifying vision, on the other hand, causes people to act in self-interested ways, making them less likely to hold themselves accountable to anything outside themselves.

How about your team? Would high-accountability behavior improve if it had a unifying set of values and a compelling vision? Are you, the leader, driving enough energy toward these important team foundations?

Discipline

Discipline refers to the establishment of rules and processes, written or unwritten, and the commitment to follow them. We tend to equate the word "discipline" with "punishment." But I urge you to consider discipline in a much broader context – as in the discipline it takes to learn a musical instrument or a trade. Discipline is a matter of leadership consistency. Setting rules and establishing procedures, and then not following them, is highly toxic to any team – it breaks down not only accountability but trust.

Accountability requires proactive, disciplined behavior. People become proactive when they work for a disciplined boss, because doing so prevents the unpleasant consequences of failure to act: having to explain oneself in reaction to the boss's inquiries. If you find that people on your team are proactively communicating and meeting deadlines, it is probably in part because you've made it clear through your good habits that you will be following up.

Employees often wonder about the boss, "Does she really mean it?" When establishing a requirement, a policy, or a critical process, does she intend to follow up, to monitor, to measure compliance? Is she organized enough, or focused enough, to keep her eyes on the ball?

Of course it is possible – and in fact, all too common – to be too rigid, squelching creativity and morale and thus productivity. But discipline doesn't have to be rigid. And a lack of discipline also ruins many promising careers.

What does good leadership discipline look like?

- **Personal organization** – The leader meets deadlines or communicates effectively about missed deadlines. The leader shows up on time, responds promptly to phone calls and emails, and completes promised tasks.

- **Process discipline** – The leader expects certain processes and systems to produce certain defined outcomes. When those processes don't work according to plan, the disciplined leader notices, calls out the failure, and works toward either changing the process or revising the expectations. In the world of a disciplined leader, there is no room for sloppy processes, sloppy measurements, or tolerance of something that's broken.

- **Follow through on consequences** – When employee or team performance is poor, or when individuals have violated team values or norms, the disciplined leader must create consequences. Of course some consequences may accrue without the leader's intervention – embarrassment, for example, or team disapproval. To be effective and fair, the consequences the boss applies must be natural, logical responses to the behavior. These can range from the boss's vague disappointment, through verbal reprimands and write-ups, to denial of a raise or promotion – and of course all the way to termination and even legal action. None of this ever requires yelling, screaming, intimidation, or public whipping. What it does require is mental toughness, and again, consistency. If, as a leader, you are unwilling to tackle tough performance issues (whether caused by personal incompetence or process failure), you'll be unable to develop an appropriate level of team accountability. Workers often complain that leaders fail to hold individuals accountable for bad performance. When you fail to create consequences, you devalue and diminish the positive contributions of your high-performing employees, eroding both their drive to excel and their sense of accountability to the team.

Learning Environment

Healthy accountability thrives in an environment of learning, rather than one of punishment and retribution. If we want our people to learn from their mistakes – so they're less likely to repeat them – we must create an environment in which people feel safe admitting they made them. When people feel repeatedly criticized for mistakes, they shut down – not a recipe for motivation or accountability.

Healthy accountability largely derives from the Plank 1 concept of "Creative Tension." As leaders, we are honest about the gap, we invite the team to probe it with us and plan our leap, we celebrate clearing every gap, and we don't rationalize shortfalls. Without having to feel bad about themselves, the team can courageously and honestly hold themselves mutually accountable for the bad and the good.

What happens in your team when things don't go right? Is there a rush to judgment? Finger pointing? High levels of stress? If so, people will tend to hide problems and avoid responsibility. If the leader instead has fostered a learning environment – in which cooperative dialog points toward continuous improvement – the team will not operate from fear.

Leadership Character

The most obvious foundational quality for team accountability is the leader's ability to hold himself accountable, and the effect of this character trait in leading others to do the same.

How comfortable are you in owning up to your own mistakes? Does your ego get in the way, or can you put it aside when an apology is called for? Does the buck really stop here? Being worthy of followers means being honest about your limitations and taking accountability for your mistakes. Remember, the leader is always in the spotlight. Any lack of integrity damages the team greatly.

> **Making It Real**
> *Grading Your Accountability*
>
> Make a list of five key tasks or projects currently being performed under your authority. Grade your level of satisfaction (A-F) with the performance of your team on these tasks or projects. If any of the grades is lower than A, consider your role in underperforming. Answer the following questions:
>
> - Does your management of accountability need to shift?
>
> - How clear have you been about resources, priorities, process, metrics, etc.?
>
> - To what extent have you created a learning, rather than punitive, environment?
>
> - What will you do differently based on what you've learned from this reflection?
>
> Evaluate the manner in which you currently "expect accountability" in your team, and consider changes you want to implement in your approach.

The Contract

Now we've established the foundation for accountability, and there is work on your team's plate for which they'll be held accountable. I suggest that all assigned work, whether routine, repetitive, or project oriented, requires a type of contract between the manager and the employee.

The quality of this contract – how clearly it defines accepted outcomes, processes, and timelines – determines to a large degree the quality of work produced under the contract. In other words, your ability to hold others accountable is largely based on how well you write the contract.

Of course we're not suggesting that a formal, written contract be developed every time a task or project is assigned (although a process document or project plan is essentially a type of contract). What we are suggesting is that the leader always be very careful, clear, and consistent in the way work is defined and assigned in their team.

The contract does several things that benefit a team:

- Defines the work in such a way that completion of the work according to high standards is more likely.

- Specifies who's accountable to whom for exactly what, leaving no one in doubt about roles.

- Defines what contract fulfillment looks like, including metrics for success.

- Provides evidence of the agreement, so that consequences for failure to perform are easier to enforce.

Let's explore the components of the contract.

What
The contract states unambiguously and comprehensively the scope of work, the intended outcomes, and how they will be measured. The contract may or may not include how the work will be done. For repetitive tasks, it might explain in detail the steps of the process. In cases where the "what" is more flexible – a change initiative, for example, or a process redesign – the leader should as much as possible leave the "how" to the discretion of the responsible parties. Doing so fuels creativity, self-motivation and job satisfaction.

Why
People who are assigned work deserve to know why the work is being done, why *they're* doing it, and how it fits into the big picture.

Who are the stakeholders who are depending on this work being performed? Why does this work matter? These are the "context" considerations we discussed in the motivation plank (Plank 5). Knowing "why" fuels not just motivation, but accountability. Wouldn't you expect someone to be more accountable for their performance when they believe the work has meaning and importance? Take the time in the contract to spell this out.

Who
The contract defines who is responsible for the work, as well as the support expected from other task or project stakeholders. The accountability for completing the work is defined across the entire team so that the person ultimately responsible for the work doesn't have to beg, borrow, or politic to get the help they need – and so the leader doesn't have to intercede to ask for help from other stakeholders.

At its best, the contract references the whole community of stakeholders and brings them together under the umbrella of "who."

Every task, every project, every process category, should roll up to an individual, regardless of how much of the work he actually performs. Having a name on a task is a powerful way to create accountability for its completion.

When
Work is too often defined in an open-ended, non-specific way. Most often, setting time frames for work is critical. In part, they establish the priority for the work. They also connect the work to other dependent tasks or projects, defining a chronological sequence for completion – and helping in yet another way to provide the motivational "shovel" of context.

In a healthy team, deadlines are explicit expectations – not wishes, preferences, or hopes. Don't set time frames for work completion unless you mean it. Will all the work be completed on time? Of course not, but explicit deadlines will ensure the highest possible batting average.

The leader should also insist on a no-surprises rule. If a project is going south, accountability requires disclosure – well in advance of the failure. And remember, you've created a learning environment, so every failure is discussed and learned from, rather than merely criticized.

If you truly can't prioritize the work – you're simply hoping the work gets done when someone has time – you can bet it won't get done at all. And no one can be held accountable, because you didn't say "when."

What If
Embedded in any work assignment is a "what if" agreement. If priorities shift, if the unexpected occurs, if I don't get the support you defined, if I simply didn't plan my time well and fell behind, what then? In many organizations, the employee tries to buck up, work harder, hope like heck that no one notices the crisis, and plow their way through as best they can.

The contract should include a discussion of possible project obstacles, and what to do about them. It should also include these understandings:

- You are just as accountable for reporting errors, challenges, and concerns as you are for performing the work.

- I don't want to be surprised by anything.

- When you bring these challenges to me, I promise we'll work rationally and calmly toward resolution.

The Priority
When assigning work, leaders can usually assume it will be added to an already full plate. Employees will tend to heap this work onto their plate and hope for the best. Without a priority discussion and agreement with you, they are likely to:

- prioritize their own work without a full understanding of the implications.
- try to get the work done while stressing over unclear priorities.
- feel that they are failing by not accomplishing everything on their plate.

In Plank 4, The Boot and the Sandal, we discussed the importance of managing the work that doesn't get done. In order to create a healthy accountability culture, we must release employees from the stress of having to do everything, and direct them toward what's most important. Managers often take the easy way out by not helping their employees with tough prioritization choices.

In the 21st century, we run tight ships; there's seldom room for fluff. It's just bad leadership to ask people to do more than what's possible.

The Agreement and Commitment
It's not a contract until both parties are signed on. So, when assigning work, the leader must invite (not assume or demand) an explicit commitment on the part of the employee to perform the work. In this way, the employee can be held accountable to their own commitments, not just yours. The employee then becomes not just a workhorse, but a partner with you in executing the work.

In all but crisis situations, it's your responsibility to ask them if they can in good faith agree to the contract – even if it's as simple as saying, "Let me know if you have any concerns." It's also your responsibility to be open to their response – open to what you might not have considered in assigning the work. The leader doesn't have to agree with or act on the other's perspective. But the leader must listen openly and be open to being influenced.

If they can't agree to the contract, they must say why. Not enough time, perhaps, or not enough training, or not enough support – these are all issues to be addressed up front.

People don't like to say no to the boss. That's why the agreement and commitment must be a central part of the contract. Don't let an employee walk away with a passive commitment, and don't let him get away with saying, "I knew we couldn't do that" after the project has failed. If an employee feels your request is unreasonable – and you haven't given him a fair opportunity to say so – he will not feel accountable to complete the work.

Executing the Contract

At this point you've created the foundation for accountability and the contract's in place. Now you must hold yourself accountable for the ultimate execution of the contracted agreement.

1. The leader must establish a consistent pattern of **follow-up**, particularly in regard to the "when" of the contract. Diligent and disciplined follow-up tells your team you really mean it – a commitment is a commitment.

Inconsistent follow-up and poor organization on your part tells your team just the opposite – when I ask for something to be done, I don't really mean it. I'm likely to shift my focus, change my priorities, or simply lose interest. Once your employees learn this lesson from you, they will have trouble unlearning it – and the precedent that sets can be disastrous.

No one likes to be micromanaged; no one performs well in the long term being micromanaged; and no manager but the most power-hungry tyrant wants to micromanage over the long term. But establishing the tone and the culture of accountability, especially with a younger or newly-formed team (as we discussed above under "Team Accountability"), may require a high level of oversight on your part until the culture has been established. Once people learn you really "mean it," they won't have to be reminded of it perpetually. But when you assign a task and then fail to follow up at all (either one-on-one or through the publication of an agreed-upon metric), you send the message that personal accountability is not a primary value for you.

2. **Status reporting** must be built in to the work. Establish how and when you want to be updated or informed on what's been accomplished, what's left to be accomplished, and any challenges or surprises encountered. This can be done through simple project planning and electronic reporting. You may only want to hear about exceptions, or you may simply want to see a green light that indicates the work is on track, a yellow light indicating potentially significant obstacles, or a red light indicating progress has stalled or stopped. Again, the goal is a culture of accountability, and a big part of accountability is communication. Tell them what you need to know and, just as importantly, what you don't need to know.

3. Be willing and able to make **adjustments**. Of course it's a rare project that makes it all the way to completion without hitches. By creating the disciplines of contract agreement and execution within the context of a learning environment, you teach your team to be resilient, alert, and adaptive.

4. At the completion of the contract, plan a debrief – what the Army calls **After Action Reviews** (AAR's). Bring the participants together to reflect on what worked, what didn't work, and what could be done better next time. This is a powerful process: it opens the team up to honest dialog; it lets them know you value their input, thus enhancing motivation and creativity; it develops collective intelligence; and of course it sets the stage for future success. By the way, the AAR should include an open assessment of the leader's performance as well.

5. And this brings us to one of the most critical and powerful tools for creating accountability – **measurement**.

It would be impossible to overstate the importance of developing a scorecard through which employees can see their own progress objectively. Of course these metrics are part of the contractual phase. We will know the work is being performed to specification when we see these defined, concrete outcomes.

Numerous management methodologies speak to this requirement of leadership. I encourage you to study the Balanced Scorecard concept as well as LEAN manufacturing to learn more about the role that disciplined measurements play in making employees more productive and more accountable.

In Plank 1, we talked about the importance of being concrete with our goals and our vision. Unless we agree on a specific set of outcomes that define "success," we can never know that we accomplished what we set out to accomplish.

If possible, every piece of work should have a measurement or defined outcome attached. What does it mean to "process customer invoices" or to "manage projects"? Often we don't create accountability because we are ambivalent or unclear about what success looks like. By failing to establish concrete measurements, accountability applies to an interpretation of success rather than to a definition. And that's not really accountability at all, is it?

Making It Real
Drafting A Contract

In the coming week, identify a significant ongoing task or a project that you've assigned (or need to assign) to one or more members of your organization. Using the contractual model (who, what, etc.) from this plank, develop a "contract" with the employee(s) involved. The contract should spell out expectations explicitly and define in-process communication and follow-up agreements. Review the contract with the employees involved. Do all you can to foster agreement and commitment, rather than compliance. Don't assume anything!

Later, discuss with the employees the impact this level of organization and communication had on the progress and/or quality of the work.

Plank 11

Develop a Process View

I think broadly about what process means to the organization

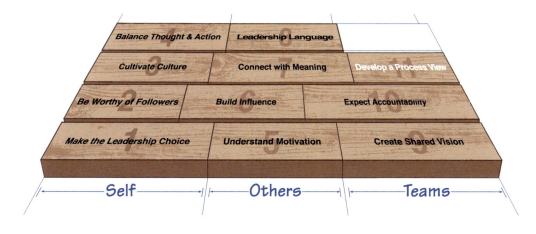

M ark was a busy man. With nine years experience in the accounting department, he was now supervising a team of 12 people. He'd recently calculated that his team had, on average, only four years of accounting experience. Half of them had been with the company less than two years.

Since Mark's arrival, the company had quadrupled in size, expanded into new product lines, and made several acquisitions. As a result of this rapid growth, the company's accounting procedures had gradually become a patchwork of loosely-coordinated activities.

The company's consolidated financial reports were due on the 15th of each month. Mark would work 16-hour days between sleepless nights to slog through three or four iterations of the reports. There were many manual entries, many facts stored only in Mark's brain, and many tweaks required. Due to his crew's lack of experience, Mark saw himself as the last line of defense against inaccuracy – but catching mistakes was demanding more and more of his time. The result was inconsistent reports that eroded the confidence of top management.

Mark's boss Ellen had expressed frustration, so far polite, about the errors in the last few reports. She asked Mark what he was doing to fix the problem. Mark blamed his team's lack of experience. "We're still suffering growing pains," he said. "We've grown so much, and there's only one of me." Ellen sighed, but grudgingly accepted the explanation.

We have to be observers, analysts, objective critics, and ultimately change agents when it comes to processes.

A few weeks later, Mark was conducting a new-hire orientation with Marta, the latest addition to his team. Marta was sharp, and Mark was glad to have her on board, but he hadn't developed a consistent approach to bringing new employees up to speed. And with the increasing workload, he had even less capacity to coach and train new hires. As he looked through his and his employees' schedules, he couldn't find any time for Marta to be trained.

In quiet despair, he suggested Marta spend some time with the Procedures and Practices Manual. He pulled his copy from the bookshelf behind him and was embarrassed to see dust fly off it. Inside the binder, random notes and documents were stuffed into the pockets. Many of the pages were discolored with age and printed with the company's old logo. Some of the procedures were clearly outdated.

Marta was polite as Mark flipped through the manual, but he worried she was questioning her decision to take this job. After walking her part way through the decaying binder, he closed it and said, "Well, this isn't going to help very much, is it?"

Marta offered a determined smile and said, "Maybe we've just discovered my first project."

Mark thought a moment. "You know, that might be a good idea down the road, but right now I just need help getting the monthly financials produced. Let me talk to David and Samantha – they're our two most experienced people; I'll ask if you can shadow them for a week or two." He forced a smile of his own and added, "You'll just have to learn like we all learned – the hard way!"

Later that week, Mark held a team meeting. Since the topic was new federal reporting requirements, Mark's boss Ellen was in attendance. He started the meeting a bit late and stumbled in delivering the information he needed to provide to the team. Several times, the meeting was interrupted while copies were made. It adjourned without a clear articulation of next steps. Mark just suggested everyone read the materials and meet again the following week.

Afterwards, Ellen followed Mark into his office and asked him how long he'd been planning the meeting. Mark said he'd scheduled it a week ago. Ellen asked Mark how he thought the meeting went.

Mark looked down at the floor and thought for a moment. Then in a quiet voice he said simply, "Chaotic and ineffective."

"Mark," Ellen said, "you know your stuff and you work hard to hold things together, but you're not strong on process – and process is critically important in every aspect of running a business, even down to running a meeting." She walked to the white board and began drawing what she described as her process for effective meetings. Mark listened attentively and asked a few questions.

"Without effective processes," Ellen concluded, "you simply can't manage the complexity of this department. By this time next month, I want you to explain to me, step by step, your process for putting together the consolidated financials. It won't be complete and it won't be perfect, but it will be a starting point to help us understand where the problems are."

On her way out the door, Ellen paused and said, "How do you think Marta will work out?"

Mark smiled and replied, "I think we'll find out – I've got a great project for her to start on."

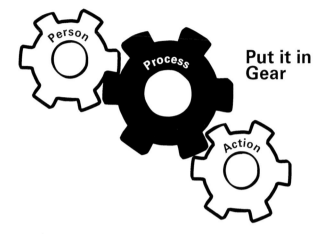

Put it in Gear

Developing a Process View

Our Leadership Platform is nearing completion. We've talked about the abilities and qualities essential for leaders to move and motivate people. We've talked about being visionary and being organized, about building relationships, and about holding ourselves and others accountable.

In Plank 10, we referred to "processes and systems" as foundational to healthy accountability. In order to get what we need from these processes, we have to be observers, analysts, objective critics, and ultimately change agents.

Plank 11 is about doing the work in a way that leans toward success. It's about balancing our focus on individual performance with an equal enthusiasm for – and curiosity about – the structures and systems that partner with the people to produce the work.

The metaphor we use for processes in the workplace is "putting it in gear." Think about the engine of a car as the potential energy of the employee. The transmission would be the mechanism for transferring that potential energy into motion. The leader's job is to "put it in gear" by allowing the energy, intentions, and capabilities of employees to flow efficiently and predictably through a set of gears to create forward motion.

What does it mean to develop a process view?

Developing a process view requires a disciplined orientation toward consistency and proactivity. It makes the leader more objective and rational, and therefore better able to steer through crises with a steady hand. The process-oriented leader creates a sense of calm, a healthy, grounded stance toward problem-solving, and an eye toward continuous improvement.

As process-oriented leaders:

- we rely on well-designed processes more than heroic efforts to get the job done.

- we focus equally on the growth of the company's processes and the growth of its people.

- we constantly strive to develop an environment of proactive, rational problem-solving.

- we repeatedly ask ourselves and our organizations this question: Could a reasonably talented employee, with reasonable effort, be expected to meet expectations by working within the systems and processes we've established?

Some of this may go against some of your treasured beliefs as a leader: Shouldn't I strive to hire only the best, not just "reasonably talented" employees? Isn't the ability to inspire an important leadership attribute? Don't I want my employees to be heroes?

Taking a process view is not inconsistent with hiring great employees, with being an inspirational leader, or with inspiring heroism. What it means is you don't depend solely on these to foster success. Even highly motivated, inspired, committed employees will fail in a process-deficient environment.

What is a process?

A process is a recipe: a planned, systematic series of actions directed toward a defined outcome. A process defines the resources, the steps, and the guidelines used in conducting the work. It thus creates a measurable result. Our day is full of processes, from making the bed to driving to work, to making macaroni and cheese. Imagine you're expected to cook macaroni and cheese, but you don't have a recipe; you're not sure of the right ingredients; you can't find the pots and pans; and you don't know how to operate a stove. That's what it's like to work in a process-poor environment. You know something needs doing, but it's much more difficult than it should be. And if results are unsatisfactory, your boss will be inclined to see you as the problem.

Taking a process view requires us to regularly dissect whatever actions are currently being employed to:

- produce a desired result
- measure success
- implement changes as necessary
- keep impacted employees in the loop

The leader who takes a process view will likely encounter numerous barriers that keep people's abilities and intentions from being translated into effective action. For example:

- redundancy
- unnecessary approvals or inspections
- poor planning
- poor communication
- lack of training
- insufficient technology or tools

The role of leadership is to remove as many of these barriers as possible. Remember: most people fundamentally want to do quality work. So when things aren't going well, it makes sense not to presume incompetence or laziness, but to search instead for process issues – usually institutional, administrative, technical, or information barriers.

You may have heard of Six Sigma, LEAN, and other programs designed to streamline processes and improve quality. Some companies need these rigorous, comprehensive programs to create competitive advantage and reduce costs. However, dramatic process improvements can often be made with simpler approaches. What's needed at the leadership level is:

The ability to observe the work first-hand
Leaders never lose sight of, or interest in, the "boot" work that produces the company's revenue (while resisting, of course, the temptation to do it themselves).

An attitude of curiosity rather than judgment
As we've seen before, the ability to suspend judgment is a key leadership attribute. Why? Because your perspective is always only one of many, and you can never be certain you have all the relevant data. For the process-oriented leader, the journey involves a thousand questions – and very few simple answers.

This creates a real balancing act for leaders – between action and reflection. Though leaders must boldly initiate action, many do so ignorantly, prematurely, or reactively. This balancing act is an art; there's no easy way to define the best approach. For a leader with a process view, the history of the business is playing out every day, under his constant study.

A slight obsession with the numbers

If you aren't interested in numbers, statistics, trend lines, and other types of analysis, you won't be in tune with processes and systems in your business. A good leader really knows her numbers – and focuses on understanding what they mean. In their landmark book, *The Balanced Scorecard,* authors Kaplan and Norton speak eloquently to the need for "leading indicators" and an approach to measurement that looks way beyond top-line revenues, simple costs, and "trailing indicators" like net profit.

In a process-rich environment, there are two kinds of "gears" that connect employees' energy to their productivity:

- Strategic "gears" – processes that create awareness, context, policy structure, broad goal definitions, flow of information, and lines of communication. If we believe it's important for employees to understand the big picture – and it is – then we need processes that deliver that big picture view.

- Management or tactical "gears" – processes that provide specific instruction and procedures, that aid in routine problem-solving, or that provide resources required for the work.

If it's not measured, maybe it's not a process. It's never enough to simply design and implement a process – it must be reviewed and measured consistently to ensure it's working.

Why Is Process A Leadership Issue?

A Process View Balances People Issues

Leaders are high on accountability, but they don't limit this attribute to human performance. Processes must also be held accountable. If customers aren't being served well, the leader asks first about the process designed to foster customer service. How can we expect people to cook tasty macaroni and cheese without a recipe?

Too often, employees are simply asked to do better and try harder. If we just ask employees to work harder before we've addressed fundamental process issues, they will just spin their gears. Before holding employees accountable, hold the system they work in accountable for providing them with a reasonable assurance of success.

As we've discussed, the leader works diligently to address issues of employee performance; he doesn't allow team vision to be compromised by individuals. But managers often experience a repeating history of failed employees. When several workers have failed at a particular role, it's more likely that the role itself is positioned for failure – due to poor processes – than that everyone who has tried it is incompetent.

By taking a process view, the leader looks for root causes. He tries, through healthy processes, to position people for success.

A Process View Makes the Organization More Objective and Intelligent

The leader's first response to failure is not, "Who screwed up?" but "What happened and why? And how can we fix it permanently?" Leaders who take this approach foster an open, affirmative, and productive dialog about mistakes and possible resolutions (related to the "learning environment" discussed in Plank 10). People are more likely to take accountability for their own actions when they're working for leaders who seek underlying causes before focusing on individual behaviors.

When members pursue solutions rather than blame, the team will think more rationally, objectively, and intelligently. By maintaining a process view, the leader literally increases the IQ of the organization.

A Process View Reinforces the Idea of "Team"

In an environment in which leadership takes a process view, the organization is more likely to think cross-functionally. The points at which team members touch their part of the process are the points where they fulfill their responsibility to the team.

Where processes are weak, individuals will just do it their way, either passively or aggressively. In this environment, employees will pass work forward without thinking critically about the how and the why of each action. The process view helps people to think globally about their work – to think of the tangible, measurable impact of their piece on the rest of the organization.

Doing more with less is a huge competitive advantage

If you are stronger in process than your competitors, you can hire out of the same talent pool and produce better results at a lower cost. Many leaders don't see this. They focus on out-recruiting their competitors for talent, while their own talent wastes away trying to work with bad – or nonexistent – processes. Go ahead and out-recruit your competitors. But here's a different way to look at it: Could I hire a person who'd been an average performer for one of my competitors, and turn them into a star performer with my company?

Why has McDonald's been so successful over the years, hiring from arguably the lowest common denominator of talent? Because everything at McDonald's has been boiled down to a science – to an efficient process. Even someone of moderate ability can perform effectively there because the processes are so nailed down. In some respects, your business should strive to do the same.

Everything Is A Process

A leader thinks broadly about what process means to the organization. Many organizations are strong in process when it comes to manufacturing activities or management of customer experiences. But every important activity in a business should be thought of as a process.

Mapping and Designing Processes

A detailed analysis of mapping business processes is beyond the scope of this book. And while I challenge you to learn more about process mapping and design, I also caution you not to make it too complicated. Here are a few steps you can take to begin developing a process view without having to earn an advanced degree in the subject:

- Ask the people who do the work to tell you what works, as well as what gets in the way. After all, they're the experts on how the work gets done. Ask them: How do we do it? Why do we do it this way? What could make the work faster, more accurate, more motivating, more customer-friendly?

- Start measuring things – simple or complicated. If you aren't doing much with metrics, start small. Measure how long, on average, it takes for a customer service rep to process an order. Measure the average length of time between the first contact with a new customer and the signed agreement. Measure the average time it takes to unload deliveries.

    A note of caution: When you begin measuring processes you haven't measured in the past, your employees may perceive it negatively. Be sure to communicate your (hopefully honest) intention to use the measurements as a process improvement tool, rather than for micromanagement. Invite employees into the measurement process. Make sure they aren't punished if the results aren't what you want.

    A note of encouragement: Many meaningful improvements in process come simply from measuring them. Why? When they know someone's paying attention, people doing the work take more pride and accountability in producing a better result.

- Cross-train your employees. It's a win-win; it reveals weak processes, and it improves accountability. When someone else is asked to do your work, you have to articulate the processes you use. This reality check can uncover old, bad habits. Imagine the experience of a new employee in your organization. If you had no experience in the company, would you have a reasonable chance of performing the work assigned in a reasonable amount of time to a reasonable standard?

Process Traps

A few common traps prevent processes from being developed in the first place, or undermine processes already in place. Leaders diligently avoid them.

The Temporary Improvement Curve

Often when a problem is identified, a quick fix is applied that works in the short term but leaves the systemic issue unresolved. A temporary improvement, resulting from simply asking people to do something differently, is not a process improvement.

Imagine your organization is having trouble getting sales people to attach receipts to their expense reports. Management responds by sending out a memo that scolds the offenders and stresses the importance of attaching receipts. The problem gets better immediately, and the manager cites his superior ability to "motivate" people. But gradually the problem reappears. Another memo is sent, followed again by a temporary improvement. And the cycle keeps repeating. Welcome to the Intermittent Nagging School of Management.

The only sustainable solution is to change the process. The current process is flawed: the expense reports are being processed without proper documentation. What if the process is changed so that expenses don't get reimbursed without receipts? Behavior would change overnight, and for good, because the sales people would feel the consequence in their wallets. This change in process would eliminate the problem – and the nagging and the frustration.

Leaders know that simply asking employees to do better within the framework of a flawed or absent process may create temporary results. But temporary results can be even worse than no results at all, because the roots of the bad habits, or ineffective processes, remain unaddressed.

Business Cycles

Developing, maintaining, and tracking processes takes time. But when times are good and business is humming and everyone is trying to keep up, process development tends to take a low priority. Likewise, when business is down, staffing tends to be tightened to save money. So once again, little time is available to design and implement process improvements to create better results.

Organizations are guilty of using both good times and bad times as excuses not to engage in process review and development, as well as application and analysis of metrics. Avoid this trap by conducting regular process reviews across the organization, regardless of whether business is good or bad.

Lack of Shared Vision

In teams where shared vision is lacking, we have discussed the tendency of individuals to act in self-interested ways. The discipline and attention required to develop and follow effective processes will suffer when individuals put themselves, rather than the team, first.

Unless they are committed to the success of the team, employees aren't motivated to understand and follow processes – let alone contribute to designing better ones. Where employees don't embrace their place in the organizational ecosystem, the process view will be lacking.

Leaders should openly and consistently invite employees to help change processes that are flawed or unproductive. The self-determination and creativity this invitation fosters can be highly motivational. In a spirit of mutual accountability, employees should be reminded that everyone suffers when poor processes are in place.

Drift Due to Exceptions

Even the best processes may need to be worked around in extraordinary cases. Unfortunately, these exceptions can quickly become the rule. Team members are likely to see even one violation of process as license to offend again.

When processes are short-circuited, leaders must acknowledge the drift and explain why the process violation was allowed. In other words, while leaders can't be unduly rigid about process, exceptions should always be rare, situational, and intentional. They should not be the result of a failure of discipline. And leaders must learn from the experience – a process that frequently needs to be worked around may be fundamentally flawed.

Lack of Metrics

A process that isn't measured is less likely to be followed. Metrics and process go hand in hand; one can't exist without the other. What good is it to define a process without knowing if the process is producing the desired result? Leaders find creative, inclusive, effective ways to measure process outputs.

Personal Power Bases

Have you ever worked on a team in which a single individual has become irreplaceable due to his proprietary knowledge of products, customers, suppliers, IT functions, or business processes? This individual often maintains leverage in seemingly laudable ways. He may be the hardest working and most knowledgeable employee in the organization – but his existence may indicate a fundamental weakness of process.

Employees can get an emotional hit for creating and maintaining a personal power base. Leaders must teach employees the danger of having significant pieces of "tribal knowledge" held by a single individual. What happens if he quits, is fired, or goes on leave? Leaders must consistently remind employees that the needs of the team supersede the power held by any individual.

Taking a process view means addressing the problem of personal power bases head on. Cross-training and process documentation are the key strategies here. The culture of a process-focused organization emphasizes quality control and consistency. It doesn't allow any one individual to hold processes hostage or exercise poor process discipline.

A Process View Enhances Leadership Effectiveness

The leader who takes a process view creates:

- more consistent, positive outcomes.
- an environment in which problem-solving and teamwork are accomplished with less stress, more objectivity, and greater speed.
- an environment in which individuals take a more global view of their inputs and outputs.
- quicker growth, learning, and improvements.
- metrics that help to understand, evaluate and manage the business.
- a competitive advantage.
- greater job satisfaction for all employees.

Making It Real
Addressing Process Issues

Analyze a deficient or nonexistent process in your organization, or a "process trap," and create a plan to address it. (For example, look for a situation in which a temporary improvement curve has occurred, and look for a way to permanently improve the result.) Your analysis/plan should include:

1. a description of how the deficiency or trap has been allowed to occur.

2. an outline of what additional information you'll need to successfully address the situation, and how you will obtain it.

3. once you obtain that information, a plan for what you will do to remedy the situation (including, possibly, delegation and expenditures), along with timelines.

4. accountability structures (i.e. what will you do to make sure these actions get completed?), including metrics to measure improvement.

As background for this project, refer to the section "Mapping and Designing Processes" in this chapter.

Plank 12

Your Leadership Legacy

I recognize that leadership growth, for me and for others, is a perpetual process requiring my focus and highest priority

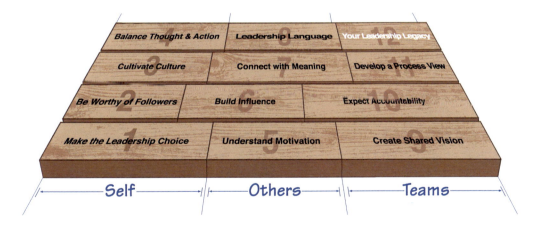

After a long management meeting, Dan followed George into his office to talk shop and debrief the meeting. The two had an excellent working relationship. George, who'd been with the company for 17 years, was about 10 years older. He saw himself as somewhat of a mentor to Dan. Dan found George to be affable, knowledgeable, and consistent.

But Dan was concerned. His friendship with George was about to be tested, he feared. George had clearly hit a plateau, while Dan's career was on the ascendancy. It was only a matter of time before student passed master on the career ladder. Despite Dan's appreciation for George and for the support he'd received, he'd heard rumblings about George being "in the way" or "not keeping up." George was competent and well-liked, but he wasn't a dynamic presence in the organization. His day seemed to have passed.

As they talked, Dan noticed for the umpteenth time the bookshelf behind George's desk. On it were several dozen books on leadership and a number of binders he'd accumulated from leadership seminars and in-house classes. All were in some state of neglect – dusty, leaning awkwardly, or faded. The books and binders once represented possibilities and energy, but the way they sat on the bookshelf now spoke of decay and stagnation.

On a whim, Dan decided to ask about the books and binders. "George, you have quite a collection of training materials there. When did you accumulate all that stuff?"

George turned and stared at the bookshelf, seeming almost surprised to see it there. He grabbed one of the books at random and flipped through a few pages. "Yes, there are a lot of good books here. I suppose it would be good for me to read them some day."

> George was a passive participant in his own development. Because of this, he had stopped getting better at his work years ago.

He grabbed a fat, dark green three-ring binder. On the front cover, the words "Critical Skills of Management and Leadership" were silk-screened in white. A smile emerged from George's face. "I remember this class – a whole week in Chicago. We had a lot of fun. The instructor was this great guy who totally energized the class. I came away feeling really close to those guys."

"How long ago did you take that class?" Dan asked.

"Oh, I'd say about 10 years ago."

"What did you learn from it?"

George thought for a minute, then opened the binder. "Let's see what I learned," he mused.

Dan reached out and pulled the binder away from George. "No, really – without looking – do you remember anything you got from this class?"

"That was a long time ago, Dan."

As they talked further, Dan realized that despite the many classes George had taken and the many books he'd bought, much of George's professional development had been wasted. George saw the classes as a pleasant diversion and a way to fulfill training obligations. He'd reacted cynically to the little bit of actual reading he'd done, discounting its value "in the real world." He'd never had a coach, he'd never sought out additional training on his own, and he'd never taken classes at the local university. George was a passive participant in his own development. It struck Dan that because of this, George had stopped getting better at his work years ago. He'd arrived at a place where he was competent and comfortable, and he'd stayed there.

Dan also realized no one had ever held George accountable for demonstrating or teaching what he'd learned in these classes. It was enough for his managers to have sent him, naively hoping George would come back an improved version of himself.

Dan concluded sadly that George was getting passed by because he hadn't taken his own development seriously, and because those who led him hadn't either.

The Path Forward

We're ready to hammer in the last plank of our Leadership Platform. But this is not an ending, but a beginning. Reading this book, even coupled with the year-long Path Forward Leadership workshop series, is the first step on a lifelong journey.

Embarking on this journey means understanding you'll never "arrive" as a leader. There is always more to learn, more to experience, more to attempt. You can't become a great leader by reading a book or taking a class, just as you can't become a great golfer in a classroom. Your development as a leader takes place over time, through the disciplined application of acquired learning to legitimate experience.

Realizing this, you commit yourself to learning leadership forever.

And thus you create the ultimate win-win for your organization. As you continue to grow, you become more effective in creating results. And you invite others to grow along with you.

This is your legacy to the organization over the long term – the quality of leadership you create around you. A true leader is less interested in being the star of the organization than in making other stars shine around them.

So, taking the path forward means two things:

- You take charge of your own leadership development.
- You take on the critical responsibility of developing other leaders.

How do you take charge of your own leadership development?

Use the Leadership Platform as an experiential guide

This Leadership Platform model can guide your future development. In fact, there's too much information in these chapters to absorb all at once. Keep the Platform as a reference tool:

- Re-read sections that apply to current challenges.

- As you ponder particular challenges or opportunities, use the Platform as a diagnostic tool. Is this an opportunity to create shared vision? Do I have an incomplete relationship that's preventing the organization from moving forward? Is there a problem with accountability?

- Follow up with others in your organization who have read the book or who attended the Path Forward Leadership workshops with you. Create a regular, ongoing dialog. You can't learn leadership alone.

- Have your employees, peers, or others in the organization read the book and compare ideas, notes, questions and intentions – and then hold each other accountable for making good on those intentions.

Seize challenging opportunities

One of the things that distinguishes the growing leader is her dissatisfaction with comfort and stability. She's always looking for the next way to challenge her abilities:
- taking on a difficult change project
- accepting an assignment that requires a temporary or permanent move
- taking on a "turnaround" of an underperforming team, department, or branch operation
- creating a winning relationship with a difficult vendor or customer

I've done all these in my career – more than once. My path, often difficult, enabled me to learn priceless lessons in leadership – without a formal business education.

These are all examples of "leaps" into an uncertain future. Leaders enjoy these leaps. Of course they entail risk, which brings us to the next point.

Embrace failure as part of the path forward

Again, the ability to rebound from failure – and more importantly to learn from it – is a hallmark of leadership. The world is full of people who go down for the count after only one punch. Leaders are persistent – and not particularly fragile.

I was once a guest at my cousin's house for about five weeks while establishing myself in a new city. My cousin was an excellent chess player. I hadn't played more than a dozen games in my life. I noticed a chess board in the living room, and on a whim I asked if he'd like to play. He warned me he was competitive and would never let me win. So we played and played. I lost 19 consecutive games to him. Finally on the 20th game, much to our mutual surprise, I won! I didn't want to celebrate too much, so I modestly pointed out that I was now 1-19. He kindly reframed: I was now 1-0. He commended me for my persistence.

Without a willingness to face into failure as a life lesson, we'll fabricate stories about our failures and move past them no better than we started. Be honest about what goes wrong – you'll always come away a wiser leader.

Create meaningful feedback loops

As leaders move up the hierarchy, studies indicate they actually get less and less feedback on their performance. But good leaders must regularly seek such feedback, and in very specific ways.

Many companies have formal "360" feedback processes, in which confidential feedback is collected from those above you, to your side, and below you in the hierarchy. If this option is available, seek it and listen carefully to what people have to say.

But formal performance evaluations are only part of the picture. Finding confidantes who will tell you the unvarnished truth about how they perceive you is even more valuable. Where can this feedback come from? From elder mentors, from bosses, from people who know you well outside the organization, from your spouse, and most courageously from those who work for you. One could argue that the people who know you best also have the most to gain from your growth – so let them in on the process. Ask them regularly to comment on the experience of working with and for you.

Read good books on the subject

People who read business books make more money and rise more quickly in their careers than people who don't, studies show.

Ten pages a day of reading is the equivalent of about ten books a year. And don't just read; have a conversation with the author: highlight passages, take notes, form your own opinions as you see fit.

Reading only business books can make you pretty boring, though, so read widely – about public affairs, history, and literature. And for balance, don't forget to read for fun. Virtually any reading informs your leadership and expands your mind. A habit of reading is by its nature a habit of personal development.

Build a network

One of the most astonishing gifts I received upon getting into the business of leadership was the profound experience of building a personal and professional network of interesting, challenging people. These people bring wisdom, encouragement and new opportunities to me in ways I never could have imagined.

How do you build such a network? Here are a few guidelines that have served me well:

- Spend more time talking to people outside your immediate area of expertise than in it.

- Pick up the phone at least once a week and invite someone to coffee. It can be anyone – an old friend you haven't seen for a while, a current or former customer, a friend of a friend, someone who intrigues you, or someone who works for a company or organization you'd like to know more about.

- Have something to offer to everyone you meet – information, questions, or additional contacts.

- Don't look too hard for what you want. If you're a good networker, good things have an amazing tendency to find you.

- On the more practical side – be a joiner. Professional and community organizations (I particularly admire Rotary International) can give you both a chance to meet people and a chance to do good in the world.

- Network internally if you work for a larger organization. Seek opportunities to learn from the best. Become part of their "circle of influence." The old aphorism is partially correct: it's about both what you know and who you know.

Be a personal visionary

We talked in Plank 1 about the importance of vision, not only at the organizational level, but at the personal level.

If you don't have a vision for yourself – about yourself – then develop one. Explore the kind of person you want to become, in and out of the workplace. Clarify your values and strive constantly to live them with integrity. Don't settle for less than you're capable of becoming. Don't live a small, safe life. Imagine what could become of your journey and what wonderful experiences could be down the pathway.

And remember to surround yourself at all times with encouraging influences!

Be coached, and be a coach

I suggest that every leader obtain the services of a professional coach at least once in their career. The experience can be remarkably clarifying, energizing, gratifying and growth-accelerating. Interview enough coaches to find one with whom you are comfortable. Choose a coach who will both support and challenge you – who will ask you tough questions, help you clarify the outcomes you want, provide wise insights and valuable resources, and nonjudgmentally hold you accountable for your commitments.

Having a regular coaching or mentoring relationship inside your organization can also be invaluable, so I suggest doing both. Working with someone outside the company has special value, however, as it is free of any hint of politics or company "persuasion."

Though not as intensive or personalized, group coaching can be highly beneficial as well. In our leadership development firm, we bring together small groups of managers from diverse companies, industries, and backgrounds to meet regularly with a professional coach/facilitator. The ability to bounce ideas and concerns off a group of non-competitive peers can have huge value.

Teaching and guiding others is also a magnificent way to develop your leadership capacities. Much of what I have learned about leadership has come from close observation and engagement with the experiences of others.

Developing your personal leadership skills is an essential part of your service and commitment to your organization. As you follow your personal path forward, you'll notice that your ability to lead others down their paths becomes more central to your role.

A legacy of influence with others

It's sometimes difficult for leaders to know how successful they've been. Many would argue that the numbers tell the story – a successful leader produces good bottom-line results. And of course we anticipate that living the Leadership Platform will enable a leader to produce such results.

But someday the numbers will be buried in the past. Your organization will have gone the way of all living things. What remains will be the legacy of the influence you had on others, and through them to succeeding generations of leaders. Your efforts to help other leaders grow could have implications for your organization and others many years into the future. For your community and world, the effect could last for centuries.

So we put the development of others near the top of our priorities. Even from a bottom-line perspective, it only makes sense. When you develop other leaders, you develop efficiency, morale, and motivation in your organization. It's no wonder execs like Jim McNerney, CEO of The Boeing Company, regard leadership development as the single most important piece of their job.

It's also one of the most immensely satisfying aspects of leadership. Through this beneficial and dynamic impact on people, you'll be building and healing spirits, families, and communities. The people you help to grow may take their new abilities and do wonderful things. You won't get the credit for these wonderful things, but you'll quietly recognize the influence you've had, and when you reach the end of your career you'll value this above just about everything else.

A system for growing leaders

Leaders aren't grown by accident. If your organization is short of quality managers and leaders, it's because top management hasn't created a system to generate them, or hasn't held that system accountable for producing.

Formal training is a critical component of this system, but by itself it's ineffective. Most of the hard work of leadership development happens inside the organization, every day. Though leadership development must be owned and championed by senior management, your Human Resources Department isn't ultimately responsible for developing leaders – you are.

In my work as a leadership consultant, I've heard executives say, "My people are letting me down," or "There just aren't enough good people out there." I like to remind them that great companies take pretty good people and make them great.

While a vigorous and effective recruitment process is an important part of the overall system, it's not good strategy to always expect to out-recruit your competition. Focus on out-developing them instead.

Even small companies can build a system for leadership development. Let's look at the building blocks.

Building Block 1: Strong corporate vision and values

Again we refer all the way back to Plank 1 – the importance of being a visionary. Why is vision so important in the context of a leadership development system? Every significant strategy and initiative in your business rests on the strength of a long-term view and a powerful sense of mission and values. So does bringing people on board and developing leaders. With a strong sense of who you are as an organization, what value you bring to market, what's most important to you, and what distinguishes you from the competition, you can select the best people and develop them the best way.

Building Block 2: A thorough and effective strategy for recruitment and selection

To attract quality employees, you can run your own campaigns, use recruiters, solicit referrals, or engage the personal and professional networks of leaders. Choose the strategy that works for you, and stick to it.

Some employers make the mistake of only recruiting during times of need. This forces the organization to hire under duress, making it more likely you'll settle for what's available quickly. A systemic approach to recruiting means you're always looking for quality – whether or not you have an immediate need.

In my estimation, selection is an even bigger challenge. Management theorist Peter Drucker estimated that businesses only make a really successful hire about a third of the time. Here are the elements of an effective selection process:

- Quality interview techniques. It's appalling how many important interviews are conducted by people who have no training in how to interview. Without a plan of attack, these untrained people tend to gravitate toward the candidate with the most obvious credentials – or the one who talks the best game – rather than the one who's truly the best choice. Take the time to train key staff on how to conduct effective experientially-focused interviews.

- Focus on talent rather than fit. Many candidates appear to have all the right experiences and talents but may not feel like a good fit for the position. Sometimes the person who turns out to the best fit for the position didn't seem to have the most relevant experience or the obvious personality characteristics during the interview.

- Use of behavioral assessments. I'm not suggesting the kinds of simple personality tests that can be pulled from the Internet – I'm talking about the robust and very effective assessments sold by a number of different companies. Choose one that is "validated" – it will be the most accurate and effective.

Building Block 3: Formal Development Processes

Formal development processes, often organized and administered by Human Resources, include:

- training programs
- performance evaluation or feedback
- career development and tracking
- succession planning

Very few companies create the necessary discipline around these efforts. Performance evaluations, particularly, should follow these guidelines:

- They should be consistent, timely, and forward looking.

- They should be delivered by a caring and competent manager who gives regular on-the-job feedback and isn't overly reliant on the formal process to communicate coaching messages. In many organizations, misguided managers "save" their feedback for the performance evaluation process. This isn't the time for surprises.

- The employee should be part of the evaluation process. He should be given the opportunity both to evaluate his own performance and to suggest how the environment could be improved to bring out his best performance.

- Evaluations should be separated from the salary review process. Salary concerns distract employees from performance discussions. Keeping the two separate also affirms that compensation must be influenced by overall company performance and labor market realities, as well as by individual performance. Finally, merging the salary dialog with the performance dialog implies that we grow and perform solely for the raise – and this flies in the face of what we know about the critical importance of intrinsic motivation.

Building Block 4: Experiential or Informal Development Processes

People develop more skills outside of the formal processes than within them. Here are a few critical things to remember.

The most important feedback and coaching are given in-flow, in real time, while events are current and fresh in both the manager's and employee's minds. This feedback can be verbal or in the form of metrics. Many leaders make the mistake of assuming a no-news-is-good-news posture with their staff. Although some employees perform well without feedback, most do not.

Effective coaching is essential to leadership development, and coaching is only effective in a spirit of growth and possibility, rather than correction or punishment. All of us flourish in the presence of people who observe us, challenge us to grow, and hold us accountable for making positive changes in our work. This one-on-one coaching may indeed be the most important part of the leadership development system. But far too often, people are given the responsibility to "coach" without the understandings and skills to do so effectively. Coaching is a complex skill set involving a multi-disciplinary understanding of human and organizational development. Leaders should be regularly trained in coaching principles and practices.

With any employee who's taking on a new challenge, it's critical to take a close sponsorship role. Whether the employee is running a meeting for the first time, taking on a difficult employee problem for the first time, or visiting customers for the first time, she needs a mentor to observe, coach, and support her. Not only will it accelerate her learning, but the mentor learns a lot about her current capabilities and growth challenges.

Building Block 5: Growth Systems

The clearer your expectations for excellence in leadership performance – and the more you hold your developing managers accountable – the more growth you'll see. If your organization is deficient in the accountability domain, your ability to develop consistent performance will suffer.

In each of the areas below, ask yourself: Is our company strong in this area today? If so, how can we expose our developing leaders to our own best practices? If not, how can we get our developing leaders the training they need to bring best practices to the organization?

- Meeting and dialog facilitation. What are our standards for running good meetings? Do we expertly facilitate open-ended dialog such as brainstorming or long-range planning?

- Process Improvement. Do we know how to systematically evaluate and improve our business processes?

- Scorecards. Are we managing data in a way that gives our managers a scoreboard on which to evaluate the effectiveness of our processes and/or the need for adjustments?

- Project Management. Does our company manage projects consistently, with the aid of a proven model?

- Critical issue resolution and decision making. Again, are these current strengths from which new leaders in our organization can learn, or are they skills that need to be developed further?

The important message here is this: developing leaders will learn from an organization's *weaknesses* as well as its *strengths*. This is why it's important to be honest about the organization's ability to lead from its own experience. You don't want up-and-coming leaders thinking your deficient processes or inefficient systems are state-of-the-art. If you have a deficiency in any of the areas above, you'll either need to hire in experience and strength from the outside, or get training or consulting to help.

As a leader, you attend to the development of growth systems as much as you attend to the development of a sales strategy or a quality improvement campaign. Great people are hard to find and hard to keep. An important measure of your leadership effectiveness is the degree to which you nurture people's talents, skills, and alignment with the company's values and mission.

As with other aspects of leadership, this means leaving ego behind. A true leader is focused on the health of the organization over and above his own ego needs. Sometimes, this means stepping aside and letting others lead. Leaders must believe with all their heart that they are enriched, not threatened, by the accomplishments and talents of others. Ultimately, your leadership will be assessed not by what you have personally accomplished, but by what the teams you have led have accomplished – and even more importantly, by the quality of relationships you've developed, and the quality of people who have chosen to follow you.

A Final Word

I wouldn't be in integrity with my own values if I didn't also encourage you to take a leadership role in the larger community. I strongly believe that what you've learned from the Leadership Platform has awesome potential to strengthen your families, your schools, your neighborhoods, your professional organizations, your churches, your cities, and your world.

What becomes evident when you choose to engage your leadership skills with the outside world is that visionary and effective leadership is desperately needed everywhere.

What are your gifts? What have you learned? And how might the world benefit from what you have to offer? How much richer might your life be if you serve those around you in the broadest possible sense?

In our Leadership Workshops, we are often gratified to hear stories of how "leaping the gap" takes on greater meaning for participants – how relationships outside the building, include those with spouses and children, are enriched by the learnings in the Leadership Platform. I challenge you to apply these lessons not just at work, but in your life as a whole. As you build your platform, you will lift others up to stand upon it – and you will find many eager to share in the safety and stability it offers them.

It's not difficult to see how hungry we are for good leadership. About half of all employees surveyed rank their bosses – and leadership in their organizations in general – as unsatisfactory. If this same deficiency exists in our public institutions and in our communities, we clearly need committed and effective leaders who choose to get involved.

This brings us full circle to Plank 1's "leadership choice." Nothing happens in the world until someone decides it is possible – and worthy of their courageous action. Leadership is a central and powerful expression of your spirit and of your best hopes for this troubled world.

We've intended to be honest with you throughout this book about the difficulties of leadership. In fact, the old saying is true: if it were easy, anyone could do it. But whether leadership is hard isn't the question. The question is whether it's important. Cynics will tell you it's not worth the effort, that things will never change, that all your efforts to change the world will be met with frustration and grief. But in the face of that attitude, leaders ask themselves: regardless of how it turns out, isn't the effort to make the world a better place simply the right way to spend my life?

Cast aside cynicism. Embrace leadership. Build your leadership platform and you'll find it filled with great people doing great work together.

Making It Real
Be a Mentor

Identify and become a mentor to current and future leaders within your team, organization, or community. Remember that someone was there for you when you were in the early stages of your development as an effective and successful leader. In fact, you can actually "change the world" through continuing to develop yourself and others…one leadership growth experience at a time.

Making It Real
Community of Practice

Continue your leadership development journey. Form or join a community of practice to discuss real-world issues that are active in your business environment. Establish a safe and open forum to exchange ideas and concerns on specific issues and opportunities that affect your organization and your own growth as a leader. Cultivate an atmosphere of trust and synergy. Meet regularly. Keep yourself and the leaders within your sphere of influence growing over time.

Making It Real
Learning Never Stops

Once a month, choose a boxed assignment from this book to revisit, review and reflect on and commit to new actions. Tweak it or expand on it, given the new realities, challenges, and opportunities you're facing today.

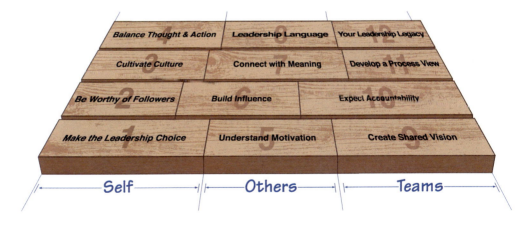

Appendix A
The Path Forward
360° Leadership Quality Assessment

Mature leaders consistently seek candid input from all levels in their organization about their management style and performance. They know that how others see them is the most critical measure of their effectiveness.

Following is a series of questions that will help you collect feedback from others about your leadership growth. The questions are drawn from The Leadership Platform concepts, and although the Platform disciplines tie directly to your real-world approach to leadership, the people providing the feedback need not have read the book in order to answer the questions.

Reproduce this "360° Leadership Quality Assessment" and share it with one or more of your superiors, peers, and subordinates. Ask them to honestly and openly respond to their perception of your leadership characteristics from their perspective.

Be sure to communicate that any and all responses will not be utilized for anything other than helping you improve in your leadership evolution. To ensure the most honest feedback, make it anonymous by asking a trusted colleague or assistant to collect the responses for you. The responses may please you, alarm you, or even cause you to get defensive… but use the information only to guide your leadership development process. If your superior wants to discuss the details further, it is a great opportunity for growth

The best approach is to launch the questionnaire early in your engagement with the book – even before you read it – and then do it again six months after you finish the book. If you consistently apply the practical concepts of the Platform, the odds are great that you will see improvement in the later responses. The Leadership Platform provides the tools for you to grow as a manager and leader in your organization and the world. For everyone's sake, use the disciplines and pass them on. Your legacy awaits.

Path Forward
360° Leadership Quality Assessment

_____
Name of Individual to be Assessed

Plank 1 – Making the Leadership Choice
- Gets out in front on key issues and is willing to accept risk to make things happen.

Consistently   Frequently   Occasionally   Rarely   Don't know or
                                                        Not Applicable

- Learns from failure and makes course adjustments effectively.

Consistently   Frequently   Occasionally   Rarely   Don't know or
                                                        Not Applicable

- Sets clear goals and pursues them with spirit and persistence.

Consistently   Frequently   Occasionally   Rarely   Don't know or
                                                        Not Applicable

COMMENTS _____
_____
_____

Plank 2 – Being Worthy of Followers
- Accepts a high level of personal accountability.

Consistently   Frequently   Occasionally   Rarely   Don't know or
                                                        Not Applicable

- Is admired for personal integrity, character, and trust-building.

Consistently   Frequently   Occasionally   Rarely   Don't know or
                                                        Not Applicable

- Leaves a positive personal "wake" behind when dealing with others.

Consistently   Frequently   Occasionally   Rarely   Don't know or
                                                        Not Applicable

- Is highly organized and meets commitments consistently.

Consistently   Frequently   Occasionally   Rarely   Don't know or
                                                        Not Applicable

COMMENTS _____
_____
_____

Plank 3 – Cultivating Culture

• Is a champion of our organization's culture – its vision, its values, and its healthy norms.

Consistently   Frequently   Occasionally   Rarely   Don't know or
                                                        Not Applicable

• Is willing to challenge long-standing beliefs and assumptions that get in the way of growth.

Consistently   Frequently   Occasionally   Rarely   Don't know or
                                                        Not Applicable

COMMENTS _____
_____
_____

Plank 4 – Balancing Thought and Action

• Spends significant time and effort developing long-term improvements in strategies, work processes and systems.

Consistently   Frequently   Occasionally   Rarely   Don't know or
                                                        Not Applicable

• Sets clear priorities, both in his/her own work and in guiding the work of others.

Consistently   Frequently   Occasionally   Rarely   Don't know or
                                                        Not Applicablele

• Effectively delegates work tasks that others could do at less cost or higher efficiency.

Consistently   Frequently   Occasionally   Rarely   Don't know or
                                                        Not Applicable

COMMENTS _____
_____
_____

Plank 5 – Understanding Motivation
• Fosters strong personal connections among teammates and co-workers.

Consistently   Frequently   Occasionally   Rarely   Don't know or
                                                            Not Applicable

• Listens to and understands the needs and aspirations of employees and teammates and strives to find "wins" for them in the work.

Consistently   Frequently   Occasionally   Rarely   Don't know or
                                                            Not Applicable

COMMENTS _____
_____
_____

Plank 6 – Building Influence
• Effectively influences others outside of his/her immediate area of responsibility.

Consistently   Frequently   Occasionally   Rarely   Don't know or
                                                            Not Applicable

• Markets ideas persistently and purposefully without being heavy-handed or authoritarian.

Consistently   Frequently   Occasionally   Rarely   Don't know or
                                                            Not Applicable

• Is willing to advocate for an idea even when it meets initial resistance from others.

Consistently   Frequently   Occasionally   Rarely   Don't know or
                                                            Not Applicable

COMMENTS _____
_____
_____

Plank 7 – Connecting with Meaning
• Builds and nurtures relationships that result in growth for both parties.

Consistently   Frequently   Occasionally   Rarely   Don't know or
                                                            Not Applicable

- Is willing to have the "tough" conversations, and conducts them effectively.

Consistently   Frequently   Occasionally   Rarely   Don't know or
                                                    Not Applicable

COMMENTS _____
_____
_____

Plank 8 – Leadership Language
- Listens to others with commitment, skill, focus, and an open mind.

Consistently   Frequently   Occasionally   Rarely   Don't know or
                                                    Not Applicable

- Clearly communicates expectations and directions.

Consistently   Frequently   Occasionally   Rarely   Don't know or
                                                    Not Applicable

- Develops quality dialog with others and in groups by using an open, questioning, and non-judgmental approach.

Consistently   Frequently   Occasionally   Rarely   Don't know or
                                                    Not Applicable

COMMENTS _____
_____
_____

Plank 9 – Creating Shared Vision
- Creates an environment of common vision, purpose and understanding among team members.

Consistently   Frequently   Occasionally   Rarely   Don't know or
                                                    Not Applicable

- Encourages and facilitates effective teamwork around problem-solving, process improvement, and project work.

Consistently   Frequently   Occasionally   Rarely   Don't know or
                                                    Not Applicable

- Is positive and supportive of our team and of other teams that depend on us.

Consistently   Frequently   Occasionally   Rarely   Don't know or
                                                    Not Applicable

COMMENTS _____
_____
_____

Plank 10 – Expecting Accountability
- Is highly productive and disciplined in directing the completion of work and the meeting of commitments.

Consistently   Frequently   Occasionally   Rarely   Don't know or
                                                    Not Applicable

- Helps team members understand priorities and deadlines, and offers support in meeting them.

Consistently   Frequently   Occasionally   Rarely   Don't know or
                                                    Not Applicable

- Implements appropriate consequences for lack of performance to clearly articulated standards.

Consistently   Frequently   Occasionally   Rarely   Don't know or
                                                    Not Applicable

COMMENTS _____
_____
_____

Plank 11 – Developing a Process View
- Focuses on making the system work better by making regular improvements in procedures, processes, training, quality assurance, etc.

Consistently   Frequently   Occasionally   Rarely   Don't know or
                                                    Not Applicable

- Solves problems in a rational, thoughtful way while avoiding "blame and shame."

Consistently   Frequently   Occasionally   Rarely   Don't know or
                                                    Not Applicable

- Uses measurements and statistics to develop an objective understanding of what's going on.

Consistently   Frequently   Occasionally   Rarely   Don't know or
                                                        Not Applicable

COMMENTS _____
_____
_____

Plank 12 – Leaving a Leadership Legacy

- Effectively coaches and mentors others to develop their leadership skills.

Consistently   Frequently   Occasionally   Rarely   Don't know or
                                                        Not Applicable

- Solicits honest and open feedback and coaching about his/her performance from others.

Consistently   Frequently   Occasionally   Rarely   Don't know or
                                                        Not Applicable

- Consistently provides scheduled formal feedback and salary reviews.

Consistently   Frequently   Occasionally   Rarely   Don't know or
                                                        Not Applicable

- Makes effective hiring and promotion decisions.

Consistently   Frequently   Occasionally   Rarely   Don't know or
                                                        Not Applicable

COMMENTS _____
_____
_____

I also want to say _____
_____
_____
_____
_____
_____
_____

Appendix B
The Path Forward Business Relationship Evaluator

1. Shared Vision and Goals	Score from 0 (lowest) to 5 (highest)
You share an articulated and common set of goals regarding the future of the team, department, or organization.	
You are able to help motivate one another through your understanding of one another's intrinsic motivations and needs.	
You seek win-win solutions within this relationship. The relationship avoids conflict brought on by real or perceived imbalances of power.	
The relationship has no "hidden agendas" – what each person wants and needs from the relationship is actively understood and acknowledged.	
You help each other set goals and establish priorities that are consistent with the organization's goals and values. You challenge choices or priorities that are inconsistent with the organization's goals and values.	
TOTAL ALL SCORES IN THIS SECTION	

2. Real Communication	Score from 0 (lowest) to 5 (highest)
You take sufficient time out of the work week to connect with one another.	
Both partners are fully present and engaged for one another. You truly listen to one another and you "seek to understand."	

Your conversations are productive and substantive – not built primarily around superficialities or trivialities.	
Your conversations are generally positive in nature. You provide a sympathetic ear but you do not share or enable the other person's victimization.	
The two of you discuss issues directly and do not triangulate through others.	
TOTAL ALL SCORES THIS SECTION	

3. Integrity	Score from 0 (lowest) to 5 (highest)
The relationship and the dialogs between you are appropriate both professionally and personally. You are civil and compassionate with one another.	
There is a high level of trust in the relationship.	
You drive one another to do your best. Competition between you for recognition, compensation, or promotions is not a destructive element in the relationship.	
Confidentialities are maintained in this relationship.	
Disagreements are acknowledged without excess emotion, and conflict is resolved effectively.	
TOTAL ALL SCORES IN THIS SECTION	

4. Growth	Score from 0 (lowest) to 5 (highest)
You provide honest and objective feedback to one another, even if no one else will.	
There is dual influence in the relationship – both parties respect the points of view of the other and are persuaded accordingly.	

You don't think too much alike – the relationship helps you challenge your mental models and grow in your critical thinking capacity.	
You help one another to keep perspective and to put aside destructive emotions.	
You each generally feel that you are better or healthier for having known one another.	
TOTAL ALL SCORES IN THIS SECTION	

TOTAL ALL SCORES (100 Possible)	

About the Authors

Jim Hessler

Jim Hessler is the Founder of Path Forward Leadership Development Services in Bellevue, Washington.

Jim gained extensive real-world leadership experience in a "bootstrap" business career after studying Music and Literature in college. He started in low-level retail work and developed into a strategic executive in one of America's largest corporations. He distinguished himself by conducting a series of successful business turnarounds, which gave him the perfect laboratory to learn his craft and test his ideas.

Along this unusual journey, Jim was struck by just how challenging the path to leadership can be. He recognized that leadership is best learned as a result of a long-term commitment, learning through one's current experiences, and working through the process of learning in the company of other seekers.

Building on his extensive experience as a business leader, Jim developed the Path Forward Leadership Workshops built on the conceptual model of the Leadership Platform. This book acts as a study guide for Workshop participants, as well as a candid, down-to-earth, and useful guide for anyone striving to understand the essential art of leadership.

Jim has been married for over 30 years and has two adult children. He lives in Bellevue Washington and can be reached at JimH@PathForwardLeadership.com.

Steve Motenko

Steve Motenko is a Harvard-educated leadership trainer and certified personal coach. Formerly an award-winning journalist, Steve is now a partner in Path Forward Leadership Development Services. He has facilitated management training experiences at Fortune 100 companies such as Boeing and Microsoft, as well as in government agencies, nonprofits, community organizations, and educational institutions across the United States. In his individual coaching practice, he supports leaders who are serious about living into their highest aspirations. Steve makes his home in paradise – Washington State's Whidbey Island – with his wife Karen and their rambunctious puppy Lucas.